Philip Ker. ...

Straightforward

Upper Intermediate **Workbook**

MACMILLAN

Macmillan Education
Between Towns Road, Oxford OX4 3PP
A division of Macmillan Publishers Limited
Companies and representatives throughout the world

ISBN: 978-1-4050-1090-0 with key edition
ISBN: 978-1-4050-1091-7 without key edition

Original design by Newton Harris Design Partnership.
Page make up by eMC design; www.emcdesign.org.uk
Illustrated by Rowan Barnes-Murphy pp12, 27, 34, 50, Fred Blunt
pp37, 80, 85, Tim Kahane pp31, 64, Joanna Kerr pp16, 52, 60, 83, Julian
Mosedale pp17, 41

Cover design by Macmillan Publishers Limited
Cover photograph by: (from left to right)
Alamy / Arco Images, Panos Pictures / Mark Henley, Lonely Planet / Eric
L. Wheater, Science Photo Library / Damien Lovegrove, Corbis / Jose
Fuste Raga / Zefa, Dean Ryan 2006, Corbis / Royalty Free, Alamy / Arch
White, Corbis / Chris Collins, Photolibrary / Jon Arnold Images, Corbis /
John-Francis Bourke / Zefa, Corbis / Matthias Kulka / Zefa

Photo research by Alison Prior.

Authors' acknowledgements
The authors would like to thank Cheryl Pelteret, Nicola Gardner and Katie
Stephens.

The authors and publishers would like to thank the following for
permission to use their material:
Extract from 'White-fronted parrots' and 'Non-nurturing cuckoos' both
taken from The Book of Lists by Amy Wallace and David Wallechinsky
(Canongate 2004), copyright Amy Wallace and David Wallechinsky 2004,
reprinted by permission of the publisher.
Extracts from The Guinness Book of Oddities edited by Geoff Tibballs
(Guinness Publishing Ltd, 1995), copyright © Geoff Tibballs 2005,
reprinted by permission of Geoff Tibballs.
Extract from www.msoucy.com, reprinted by permission of the author.
Extract from 'Interview with Lady Helen Taylor' by Hilary Alexander first
published in The Daily Telegraph 10.04.06, reprinted by permission of the
publisher.
'The Unicorn in the Garden' taken from Fables for Our Time and Famous
Poems by James Thurber (Harper Colophon, 1940), copyright © James
Thurber 1940, reprinted by permission of The Barbara Hogenson Agency
Inc on behalf of the James Thurber Estate.
Extract on page 28 from Oxfam GB website www.oxfam.org.uk (2006),
reprinted by permission of Oxfam GB, Oxfam House, John Smith Drive,
Cowley, Oxford, OX4 2JY, UK. Oxfam GB does not necessarily endorse any
text or activity that accompanies the materials.
Extract from www.arbourvale.slough.sch.uk, reprinted by permission of
Arbour Vale School.
Extract from www.richardhill.co.uk, reprinted by permission of the author.
Extract from www.historic-uk.com, reprinted by permission of the
publisher.
Extract from Girl with a Pearl Earring by Tracy Chevalier (HarperCollins,
1999), copyright © Tracy Chevalier 1999, reprinted by permission of the
publisher.
'If Only' by Fred Hobbs copyright © Fred Hobbs 1999.
Extract from www.greenpeace.org, reprinted by permission of the publisher.

Although we have tried to trace and contact copyright holders before
publication, in some cases this has not been possible. If contacted we will
be pleased to rectify any errors or omissions at the earliest opportunity.

The authors and publishers would like to thank the following for
permission to reproduce their photographic material:
p4 Cartoon Stock, p6 Penguin Group, p7 Cartoon Stock, p9 (l) Alamy/
Vario Images GmbH & Co. KG, p9 (r),Alamy/Image Broker, p10 Getty
Images/Photographers Choice, p11 Cartoon Stock, p13 Getty Images/AFP,
p14 Cartoon Stock, p14 Corbis/Hal Beral, p15 (bl, br) Alamy/Arco Images,
p15 (cl) Getty Images/Photographers Choice, p15 (cr), Alamy/Peter
Fakler, p15 (tl), Alamy/LMR Group, p15 (tr) Nature Picture Library/Steve
Knell, p18 Alamy/Peter Barritt, pp 19, 20 Cartoon Stock, p21 (bl) Alamy/
Profmedia Int sr-o, p21 (tr) Alamy/Pictorial Press, p22, Corbis/Andrew
Brookes p22, Alamy/Robert Harding Picture Library, p23 Cartoon Stock,
p24 Getty Images/Time & Life Pictures, p25 (br) Alamy/David South,
p25 (l) Cartoon Stock, p26 Cartoon Stock, p27 (tl) Getty Images, p27 (tr)
Science Photo Library, p28 Alamy/Visual Arts Library, p29 Cartoon Stock,
p29 Brand X Pictures, p30 (bl) Corbis/B Mathur/Reuters, p30 (cr) Harper
Collins Publishers, pp32, 33 Michael Soucy, p34 (r) Cartoon Stock, p36
Getty Images/Time & Life Pictures, p37 Getty Images/Hulton Archive,
p38 Cartoon Stock, p40 Alamy/Angela Hampton, p43 Cartoon Stock, p45
Getty Images/Dave Benett, p46 Cartoon Stock, p47 Corbis/Reuters, p48
Alamy/Stockfolio, p49 Cartoon Stock, p53 Kobal/Marvel/Sony Pictures,
p57 (br) Dennis Erofeyev Photography, p57 (cl)
Alamy/Content Mine Int, p59 Cartoon Stock, p62 (l) (r) Oxfam, p67 (b)
Corbis/Mou Me Des Jeux), p67 (t) Kobal/Lucas Film/20th Century Fox,
p69 Alamy/Stan Kujawa, p70 Cartoon Stock, cartoon by Tony Hall, p71
Kobal/20th Century Fox, p72 Corbis/RF, p74 Pixtal, p75 (l) Corbis/Frank
Trapper, p75 (l), Cartoon Stock/Fran p76, Corbis/Hulton Archive, p80
Alamy/Olga Kolos, p81 Alamy/Popperfoto, p82 Kobal/Mirimax/Universal,
p83 (l) Getty Images/Stone, p83 (r) BBC Images/Courtesy of Duncan
Hayes, PFD Agents, p76 Cartoon Stock/Fran.

Printed and bound in Thailand

2014 2013 2012
11 10 9 8

Contents

Writing

Useful language to improve your writing p76
Short story: extract from *Anna Karenina* by Leo Tolstoy p90
Key pi

1A | Consuming passions

LEISURE INTERESTS

1 Complete the text with the words in the box.

> aficionado   crazy   get   got   give   into
> keen   obsessed   passion   take

How to ... have a hobby. In 10 easy steps.

1 You want to do something in your spare time.

2 So you decide to _____ up a hobby.

3 You'll probably be introduced to it by a friend who's already _____ on it.

4 You _____ it a try, and immediately _____ a taste for it.

5 Next thing you know you've _____ the bug and you're buying all the equipment.

6 Gradually your hobby turns into a _____.

7 You read magazines and books about it, you can't talk about anything else and your friends accuse you of being _____.

8 You're so _____ it that you take time off work to dedicate to it.

9 Soon you've become a complete _____, an expert in your field.

10 It's not just something you do in your spare time anymore. You're _____ about it. It's a way of life.

www.CartoonStock.com

VERB FORMS REVIEW

2 Find and delete one unnecessary word in each of the sentences.

1 She's does a lot of sport in her spare time.
2 We've has been taking part in a lot of competitions lately.
3 The winners were be given generous cash prizes.
4 They're is coming with us to the ghost festival next weekend.
5 He had have competed in a number of international tournaments.
6 I've always was been interested in photography.
7 We did went mushrooming at the weekend.
8 A new paintballing course was being been built.

3 Match the statements 1–8 to a response in the box.

> Does he?   Have you?   Were they?   Did it?
> Had she?   Has she?   Was I?   Are you?

1 You were always playing chess with your dad when you were a kid.
2 Did you know that Joanna's just taken up Thai kickboxing?
3 Dave spends hours and hours in the garage playing with his model train set.
4 I've just been asked to take part in a half marathon.
5 Helen was really tired last night as she'd just come back from a long hike in the mountains.
6 Did you know that mum and dad were thinking about buying a mobile home last year?
7 Our cat won the best-behaved cat award in last week's show.
8 I'm taking a diving course at the local swimming pool next month.

🔘 DICTATION

4 🔘 **01** Write the sentences that you hear.

1 _____
   _____

2 _____
   _____.

3 _____
   _____?

4 _____
   _____

1B | Paintballing

NEGATIVES & QUESTIONS

1 Make the sentences negative.

1 Paintballing is dangerous.

_____.

2 It teaches people to use firearms.

_____.

3 Paintballers often have violent tendencies.

_____.

4 It has been used for military training purposes in a
number of countries.

_____.

5 Players have been killed in paintballing accidents.

_____.

6 Paintmarkers look like real guns.

_____.

7 Paintballing was very popular ten years ago.

_____.

8 Paintballing started out as a game.

_____.

2 Complete the dialogue with the correct form of the verbs
in brackets.

A: Steve, you've got an unusual hobby, what exactly
(1) _____ (be) it?
B: Well, it (2) _____ (be) so unusual, you know.
There are millions of people out there who do it every
day. We just (3) _____ (hear) about it that much.
A: So, how (4) _____ (get) you started?
(5) _____ (do) you it as a child? I mean, who
(6) _____ (give) you your first Lego set?
B: I was 8 years old when I built my first personalized
model. I mean, I (7) _____ (follow) any
instructions or anything, I just made it up myself.
A: And what (8) _____ (be) it a model of?
(9) _____ (get) you any help to make it?
B: My dad didn't actually help me, but he did give me a
lot of encouragement. It was a very ambitious model
– a copy of a bridge over the river in our town. I
(10) _____ (know) at the time, but my dad
entered it for a competition. I (11) _____ (find)
out about it till a few weeks later, when a letter came
through the post telling me I'd won!
A: And that was just the beginning! What
(12) _____ (work) you on at the moment?
B: A ten-foot replica of the Eiffel Tower.

SAYING NO

3 Complete the responses with the phrases in the box.

Are you kidding?   I'm afraid not   I wish I could
Not especially   Not exactly   Not to my knowledge

1 **A:** Will you be able to make it to the party on Friday?

B: _____, I've got to be in London for a
meeting.

2 **A:** Has Jamie signed up for the Star Trek convention
yet?

B: _____. Or at least he hadn't when I
last looked.

3 **A:** Did you tell Jane about the problem with the car?

B: _____ I wouldn't dare! I was leaving
it to you to tell her!

4 **A:** Did you enjoy the outing?

B: _____. I mean it was OK, but it isn't
really my kind of thing.

5 **A:** So you made this yourself, did you?

B: Well no, _____. I mean I bought the
parts and I just had to assemble it.

6 **A:** Are you going to the match on Saturday?

B: _____! But I've got to go to my
mother-in-law's for lunch. It's her birthday.

TRANSLATION

4 Translate the text into your language.

Have you ever found yourself saying, 'I'll do my best', 'I'll
get back to you' or even 'Yes, of course,' when what you
really wanted to say was 'no'? 'No' is one of the shortest
words in the English language, but it is also one of the
most difficult to say. Remember, if you say it politely, with
a smile, it's much easier in the long run than agreeing to
something you really don't want to do.

1c | Autograph hunters

TIME ADVERBIALS

1 Complete the text with the words in the box.

afterwards	begin	end	finally	first	while

To (1) _____ with, I didn't really take much notice of them, but after a (2) _____ I started to listen to their songs and liked them. Then a friend offered me a ticket to one of their concerts. At (3) _____, I didn't really want to go. The ticket was too expensive, but in the (4) _____, my friend persuaded me and (5) _____ I was hooked! I started going to all their concerts, and then after months of chasing them around I (6) _____ got their autographs!

2 Match each of the words to two words or phrases from the text in exercise 1.

1 initially
2 eventually
3 subsequently

VOCABULARY FROM THE LESSON

3 Choose the best word a–c to complete the sentences.

1 We were allowed to go _____ to meet the stars.

   (a) background   (b) backhand   (c) backstage

2 I don't usually give autographs, but I'll make an _____ for you.

   (a) elimination   (b) exception   (c) overreaction

3 I was watching the limousines draw up when I felt a tap on my _____.

   (a) shoulder   (b) waist   (c) ankle

4 Huge crowds turned up for the movie _____ at Leicester Square in the hope of catching a glimpse of the stars.

   (a) show   (b) viewing   (c) premiere

5 Can you please add your _____ at the bottom of each page of the contract?

   (a) sign   (b) signature   (c) autograph

6 She really wasn't surprised when he refused point _____ to sell.

   (a) completely   (b) totally   (c) blank

7 Why don't you call the shop to ask if they've got any in _____?

   (a) display   (b) stock   (c) trade

8 Both autographs and signed photos sell at incredible prices. Especially the _____.

   (a) later   (b) last   (c) latter

4 Complete the sentences 1–7 with the phrases a–g.

1 He's gone to the main square to swap
2 If you don't do something to liven up
3 People often dedicate
4 She set up
5 The government is hoping to trade
6 Unfortunately, I won't be able to attend
7 You really ought to display

☐ a a lot more with South American countries.
☐ b football stickers with other collectors.
☐ c next week's training day.
☐ d the company with the money she made from car boot sales.
☐ e their books to family and friends.
☐ f this party, I'm going.
☐ g your collection on the walls of your house.

TRANSLATION

5 Translate the text into your language.

Alex-Li Tandem sells autographs – a small blip in a huge worldwide network of desire. It is his business to hunt for names on paper, collect them, sell them and occasionally fake them, and all to give people what they want: a little piece of Fame. But what does Alex want? Only the return of his father, the reinstatement of some kind of all-powerful benevolent God-type figure, something for his headache, three different girls, and the rare autograph of forties movie actress, Kitty Alexander.

1D | Collectors

WHAT CLAUSES

1 Complete the sentences 1–6 with the phrases a–f.

A
1 What always happens is …
2 What he really believes is …
3 What I don't understand about him is …
4 What I like most about my job is …
5 What I really hate most of all is …
6 What I've always wanted to do is …

B
- ☐ a the hours. They're very flexible and I can even work from home at times.
- ☐ b his attitude to his family. He really doesn't seem to want to spend any time with them.
- ☐ c the two of them end up fighting and arguing over who is the best.
- ☐ d having to clean up afterwards. It's so boring!
- ☐ e find a way to make money with my hobby. That'd be really great!
- ☐ f that if you really want to do something, you'll find a way to do it.

2 Insert *is* in the sentences.

1 What you don't understand he's happy enough as he is.
2 What you need to do find something to occupy your time.
3 What Bob wants a bit of peace and quiet after a hard day at work.
4 What you could do arrange for both of you to go out with friends.
5 What your friends can do suggest some other activities outside the house.
6 What you really need to do stop worrying!

3 Rewrite the sentences using a *what* clause.

1 I was just telling Bob that he should take up a hobby.

_____.

2 He really needs to get out of the house sometimes.

_____.

3 I've suggested he should give fishing a try.

_____.

4 I mean, it's very relaxing and it would get him out in the fresh air.

_____.

5 Bob thinks it would be boring.

_____.

6 He'd prefer to stay at home and read a good book.

_____.

7 He says I'm obsessed with unnecessary hobbies.

_____.

EXPRESSIONS WITH *THING*

4 Complete the sentences with a word in the box.

about	another	in	for	good	past	those

1 I started out buying a couple on holiday, and then one thing led to _____, and before I knew it, I had a houseful of them!

2 She'd always had a thing _____ pigs. I don't know why. She's even got a cushion in the shape of a pig.

3 He used to love collecting model trains, but that's a thing of the _____. He's into boats now.

4 They're forever starting new collections. I've no idea what the _____ thing is at the moment!

5 I can't see the attraction in collecting things. Why do people do it? It's expensive, _____ one thing.

6 She's totally obsessed by her garden gnomes. It's a _____ thing they've got a big garden.

7 What he gets out of it is a total mystery to me. It's just one of _____ things.

© Mike Baldwin / Cornered
www.CartoonStock.com

Bob loved the outdoors. Wound up with quite a collection.

DICTATION

5 🔊 **02** Write the conversation that you hear.

_____

_____

_____

_____

_____

1 | Reading

1 Read the article and match the paragraphs 1–6 to the headings a–f.

- ☐ a How it started
- ☐ b How to play
- ☐ c World Championships
- ☐ d Sudoku on TV
- ☐ e The meaning of the word
- ☐ f The popularity of the game

2 Read the article again and decide if the sentences are true (T) or false (F).

1 Anyone who wanted could take part in the championship games in Lucca. _____

2 Most of the best Sudoku players are men. _____

3 No special skills are required to do Sudoku puzzles. _____

4 Sudoku magazines are extremely popular in Japan. _____

5 Sudoku was invented in Switzerland. _____

6 The first country in the world where people got the Sudoku bug was Britain. _____

7 The game of Sudoku is not always called Sudoku. _____

3 The sentences a–f were cut from the end of each paragraph of the article. Match the sentences to the paragraphs 1–6.

- ☐ a According to the rules of the game, only games with one solution are permitted.

- ☐ b However, she practises for two hours a day and is a regular visitor to the top Sudoku websites.

- ☐ c Other names include 'Squared Away', 'Single Number' and 'Nine Numbers'.

- ☐ d The magazine is now hoping that its new game, Kakuro, will prove to be equally popular.

- ☐ e The puzzle was an overnight sensation and Sudoku had become a household word.

- ☐ f Unlike crosswords, anyone can do it.

4 Complete the sentences with one word.

1 If something (a business, for example) takes _____, it becomes successful or popular very fast.

2 If you pick _____ on something, you react to something that you have noticed.

3 If you fill something _____, you complete it by adding information.

4 If you get _____, you have a high enough score to pass.

5 If you work something _____, you solve a problem.

6 If you turn something _____ something else, you transform or change it.

7 If you slip _____, you make a mistake.

Find these phrasal verbs in the article to check your answers.

5 Which of the statements is closest to what you think about Sudoku?

1 I'm a real Sudoku fan and love doing the puzzles.
2 Sudoku is quite fun but I can't understand why people get so obsessed with it.
3 I might give Sudoku a try one of these days.
4 I've got better things to do with my time than play games like Sudoku.

🔘 Read & listen

6 🔘 03 Listen to Reading 1 *All you need to know about … Sudoku* on the CD and read the article again.

All you need to know about ... Sudoku

1   Called 'the fastest growing puzzle in the world', Sudoku was virtually unheard of in Europe until a few years ago. The craze first took off in Japan over twenty years ago and the Japanese now buy hundreds of thousands of Sudoku magazines every month. When a British newspaper began publishing the game in 2004, its sales rocketed. Other newspapers were quick to do the same. Reports on CBS and other TV news channels picked up on the craze and suddenly Sudoku was everywhere. There are now Sudoku magazines, Sudoku books and games for mobile phones.

2   The rules of Sudoku are simple enough, but the puzzle itself can be fiendishly difficult to solve. The board has nine rows of nine squares and it is divided into nine boxes of nine squares. The player is given a few numbers to start with (no more than 32) and then has to fill in the grid so that each row and each box contains the numbers one to nine once only. The puzzle requires no mathematical skill – it is a test of pure logic and concentration.

3   The first Sudoku World Championship was held in Lucca, Italy over two days in March 2006 and was won by Jana Tylova, a 31-year-old accountant from the Czech Republic. The participants, who came from 22 countries, had to get through preliminary qualifying competitions in their own countries before making the journey to Lucca. The 85 qualifiers began with straightforward Sudoku grids before attempting more difficult variations, with the fastest person to work out the solution winning the most points. Tylova, the only woman in the top 18 competitors, was unable to explain the secret of her success.

4   Sudoku was probably inspired by the work of the eighteenth century Swiss mathematician, Leonhard Euler, but the puzzle as we now know it was designed by Howard Garns, an American architect and puzzle constructor. His game was included in a New York puzzle magazine, but it was a Japanese magazine, *Monthly Nikolist*, that changed some of the rules and turned Sudoku into what it is today.

5   Sudoku is an abbreviation of a Japanese phrase that means 'the numbers must be single'. In Japan, the word Sudoku is the copyright of the publishing company, Nikoli, so the puzzle is sometimes referred to by other names such as 'Number Place', which was its original name in America.

6   In 2005, the first Sudoku show on TV was broadcast by the Sky channel in the UK. Nine teams of nine players (including celebrities) took part in the studio while viewers at home could also join an interactive competition. To publicize the show, Sky TV carved a huge Sudoku grid, almost 100 square metres, on a hill overlooking a motorway in the west of England. Unfortunately, the designers of the giant puzzle slipped up, as there were over one thousand possible solutions.

2A | Wildlife

ADJECTIVES

1 Match the words in the box to their definitions 1–8.

> aggressive   cold-blooded   cute   ferocious
> inquisitive   obedient   playful   tame

1 keen to learn about a lot of different things _____
2 attractive, usually small, and easy to like _____
3 doing what a person, law or rule says you must do _____
4 trained not to attack _____
5 quick to attack _____
6 violent and able to cause serious injury _____
7 deliberately cruel and showing no emotion _____
8 lively and full of fun _____

2 Complete the sentences with a word in the box in exercise 1.

1 Although rats are relatively small, they can be very _____ and should be approached with caution.

2 Tigers, panthers and lions are _____, wild animals. They are not suited for domestic life and should never be kept as pets.

3 Man is the most _____ killer in the animal kingdom, sometimes even doing it for pleasure.

4 Small children are naturally _____ and parents need to be patient in answering the thousands of questions they are forever asking.

5 If a large dog is not _____ to its owner, then it is a potential danger.

6 Children are often attracted to animals that look _____ in pet shop windows.

7 The deer in the park have become so _____ they will approach people and even help themselves to their picnics.

8 Take care when walking behind a young horse: a _____ kick could actually cause a serious injury.

PRESENT HABITS

3 One of the three options in italics is not correct. Find and delete the phrase which is **not** correct.

The saltwater crocodile is the world's largest living reptile. Males (1) *will often grow / often grow / are often growing* to over five metres, whilst females are usually smaller, measuring around three metres. They have a reputation for being man-eaters, and although they usually feed on fish and crustaceans, they (2) *will also attack / have been known to attack / are often attacking* larger animals, including people. They are a particular danger in Northern Australia where there are several attacks every year. The local authorities (3) *will forever issue / are forever issuing / keep issuing* warnings and safety guidelines, but people (4) *will constantly ignore / are constantly ignoring / keep ignoring* them, with dramatic consequences. Fishermen (5) *will often feed / often feed / are often feeding* fish scraps to the crocodiles and this has made them even more dangerous, as the crocodiles (6) *have come / are always coming / keep coming* back for more.

TRANSLATION

4 Translate the text into your language.

Nile crocodiles, although physically capable of killing humans, can be very gentle with their own babies. Newborn crocodiles are tiny, weighing no more than 100 grams. In order to protect them when they come out of their shells, their mothers will place them gently into a pocket inside their enormous mouths. Then they will carry the babies to the water where they will proudly show them to their fathers.

2B | Animal rights

VERB IDIOMS

1 Replace the verb idioms in italics with a phrase in the box.

> accept   explaining   interrupting   make sense   misunderstood   saying 'no' to

1 I wish you would stop *butting in on* the conversation! It's really annoying!
2 I'm sorry, no matter how many times you explain it to me, it just doesn't *add up*.
3 Have I completely *missed the point* or do you really mean you're happy to do it?
4 There seem to be one or two things here that need *clearing up* before we go any further.
5 Look, you're just going to have to *face* it. They're not going to give you the job and that's that.
6 I've put up with about as much as I can take, but I'm definitely *drawing a line at* that!

2 Choose the correct verb idiom to complete the sentences.

1 He wasn't found guilty of the crime, because all the evidence just didn't *clear up / add up.*
2 We're going to have to *face / clear up* the fact that we aren't wanted.
3 They had *missed the point / drawn a line* and were absolutely refusing to go any further.
4 It was obvious that he had totally *cleared it up / missed the point* and didn't know what was going on.
5 Just as I was coming to the best part of the story he *butted in / added up* and stopped me in mid-flow.
6 It took us ages to explain what had gone wrong, but in the end we managed to *draw a line / clear it up.*

EXPRESSING OPINIONS

3 Complete the opinions with a word in the box.

> ask   concerned   convinced   don't   honest   personally   think   wrong

A

1 I may be _____ but aren't humans more important than animals?

2 If you _____ me, keeping pets is a waste of time and money.

3 As far as I'm _____, dogs are dirty animals and shouldn't be allowed in public places.

4 I'm absolutely _____ that pets grow to look like their owners.

B

☐ a I really _____ think there's any need to be so extreme.

☐ b Frankly I _____ it's the other way round.

☐ c To be perfectly _____, no. We do far more harm than all other species put together.

☐ d _____, I think they have a role to play as companions for elderly people.

4 Look at the sentences in exercise 3 again. Match an opinion in A to a response in B.

🌐 DICTATION

5 🌐 **04** Write the text that you hear.

_____

_____

_____

_____

_____

"The foxes in this area seem to have adapted well to urban life"

2c | Companions

PAST HABITS

1 Rewrite the sentences with the words in brackets.

1 I remember that my grandmother had a beautiful garden. (*used to*)
2 She spent hours in her garden in summer, watering the plants and tending the flowers. (*would*)
3 She didn't like us playing near the flower beds. (*used to*)
4 So she built a special playground where we spent hours and hours every holiday. (*would*)
5 We loved that playground and I was really sorry when she moved into a smaller house. (*used to*)
6 She still had a garden, but it wasn't so big and on our weekly visits we played inside the house instead. (*would*)

2 Find and correct four mistakes in the verbs in italics.

Famous British Eccentrics # 18

Lord Rokeby decided that he would like to spend all his life near or in water. He (1) *would spend* hours in the sea off the Kent beaches, and his servants often (2) *used to have to* drag him out on to dry land, unconscious. As he got older, at his country home, he (3) *used to have* a vast tank built with a glass top, had it filled with water and (4) *used to spend* all day floating in the water. He once (5) *would grow* the most enormous beard. He (6) *would be* very proud of it. It (7) *used to hang down* to his waist and spread out on the surface of the water. He (8) *would take* his meals in his pool, to the embarrassment of his family. His obsession with water was so great that he (9) *would drink* great quantities every day. He (10) *used to live* to be 88, so he was a good advertisement for the health-giving properties of water!

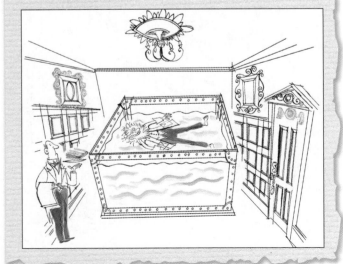

STRONG REACTIONS

3 Look at the dictionary definition and complete the examples.

> **mad** /mæd/ adj ★ ★
> **1** very silly or stupid: CRAZY **sb must be mad to do sthg** *mainly spoken* used for saying that someone is doing something very stupid.
> **2** [never before a noun] *informal* angry. **drive sb mad** *informal* to make someone feel extremely angry, upset or bored **go mad** *informal* **1** to become mentally ill **2** to become crazy because you are so bored, upset etc.
> **like mad 1** very quickly and with great effort
> **2** a lot
> **3** in a way that you cannot control or stop.
> **mad about/on sth** *informal* very enthusiastic about something

1 Dad _____ mad when he saw the mess.
2 He _____ me mad the way he keeps criticizing me all the time.
3 I would _____ mad if I had to live with him.
4 My kids are mad _____ computer games.
5 We had to work _____ mad to finish the job before the weekend.
6 You _____ be mad to sell that beautiful house.

4 Choose the best word to complete the sentences.

1 He's usually really even-tempered, but when he does get angry, he really *loses / blows* his top.
2 I don't usually get worked *up / out* about problems.
3 And whatever you do please, please try not to *lose / blow* your temper.
4 You what? You paid £5,000 for that. You need your *head / top* examined!
5 When she saw what had happened to the window she was absolutely *lunatic / livid*.
6 He's mad, totally and completely *round / on* the bend.
7 You'd have to be *totally / complete* insane to even consider doing that!

🔘 DICTATION

5 🔘 **05** Write the conversation that you hear.

_____

_____

_____

_____

_____

2D | Working animals

BE/GET USED TO

1 Choose the correct verb form to complete the sentences.

1 I don't think I'll ever *be / get* used to the way he treats his dogs.
2 I was brought up on a farm so *I'm / I'm getting* used to working with animals.
3 I've lived here for three years but I still haven't *been / got* used to the heat.
4 We prefer it if volunteers *are / get* already used to working with the blind.
5 I hate having to get up so early, but my husband *is / gets* used to it and says he loves it.
6 It took me a long, long time to *be / get* used to my new way of life.

2 Complete the text with *are used to*, *get used to* or *used to*.

The makers of virtual pets claim that the toy helps children (1) _____ the responsibilities involved in looking after a real pet. I'm not so sure. My kids (2) _____ have one when they were smaller but their interest in them disappeared pretty fast, and they soon got bored. Much the same thing (3) _____ happen with our real pets when I was a kid. But now a new virtual pet has appeared in the shops and we're going to try again. We haven't had it very long but we (4) _____ having it around already. Its attention-seeking beep can be pretty annoying to start with. It (5) _____ wake us up in the middle of the night, although you soon (6) _____ it. The kids love it. The new version is much more responsive, much more fun than the one we (7) _____ have and I highly recommend it. It may not teach the kids to be more responsible, but it certainly keeps them happy on long car journeys. If your kids (8) _____ playing with other pocket-sized computer games, then they'll love the new virtual pocket pets. And if you (9) _____ not _____ them – watch out, these pets can be pretty addictive!

COLLOCATIONS WITH GET

3 Rewrite the sentences with the correct form of the expressions in the box.

> get along   get around   get in touch with   get fat
> get involved with   get on with it

1 I first started doing voluntary work when I was at university.

    _____.

2 To start with, I didn't really have a very good relationship with our new neighbours.

    _____.

3 Stop wasting time and just do what you've got to do!

    _____!

4 Travelling by car in the centre of town can be quite stressful with all the traffic jams.

    _____.

5 I'll call you as soon as I hear any news.

    _____.

6 I've been doing loads of exercise but I still seem to be putting on weight.

    _____.

4 Rewrite the text by replacing the word *got* and making any other necessary changes.

> You think you've *got* problems? I've *got* problems! This morning I *got* a big breakfast, and *got* to work a little late. I *got* into an argument with the boss, and then *got* fired. When I *got* back home I *got* a call from my wife, who said it was time we divorced. So I *got* in touch with my lawyer, who told me he'd *got* an urgent appointment, but I *got* the impression he was lying. Just as I thought things had *got* as bad as they possibly could, I *got* …

5 Can you continue the story in exercise 4 with any more *get* expressions?

TRANSLATION

6 Translate the sentences into your language.

1 Things definitely aren't what they used to be.
2 You'd better get used to it, because it's not going to change.
3 As soon as we're used to doing one thing, we have to learn another.
4 That's one thing I'll never get used to doing.
5 We never used to, but we get on quite well now.
6 I've never really got used to being married and getting called 'Mrs'.

2 | Reading

1 Use a dictionary to find the odd word out in the box.

> beak   chick   compost   hatch   incubate
> lay (an egg)   nest   wing

2 Explain the words in italics in your own words.

1 His ideas were completely *bird-brained*.
2 I won't listen to your *bird-brained* ideas any longer.
3 Even a complete *bird brain* could answer that question.
4 Stop behaving like a *bird brain* and do something intelligent with your life.

3 Read the article. Which birds A–F:

1 build their nests near sand?
2 have to care for themselves as soon as they are born?
3 lay an egg in another bird's nest?
4 live together as a threesome?
5 lock themselves away for a few months?
6 place a stone at the female's feet?

4 Match the explanations a–f to the actions 1–6 in exercise 3.

☐ a because the males do not want to separate.
☐ b because they are abandoned by the parents.
☐ c in order to attract her.
☐ d in order to avoid dangerous animals.
☐ e so that she doesn't have to look after it herself.
☐ f so that they can use it to change the temperature of their eggs.

5 Find words in the article that match the definitions 1–7.

1 moves forward while turning over and over (bird A)
2 make something move quickly and suddenly (bird C)
3 bringing food up from your stomach back into your mouth (bird C)
4 look like (bird D)
5 covering something with a layer or pile of things (bird E)
6 not consider something or not let it influence you (bird E)
7 closes a container or space by covering it with something (bird F)

6 Explain the proverbs in your own words.

1 A bird in the hand is worth two in the bush.
2 Every bird loves to hear himself sing.
3 The early bird catches the worm.

🔊 READ & LISTEN

7 🔊 **06** Listen to Reading 2 *Bird Brains* on the CD and read the article again.

"I love a scary film"

Bird Brains

When the male **Adele penguin** (A) is looking for a mate, he takes his pick from a colony of more than a million. Having made his choice, he needs to impress the female bird he has selected. In order to do this, he finds a suitable stone, rolls it over to the female and hopes that she will accept his gift. If he's in luck, the two birds will stand next to each other, breast to breast, sing loudly and make a lot of noise with their flippers flapping. If the male fails to impress with his stone, he will have to be a bit less choosy next time. With so many other males also rolling stones around the place, he may also find that stones are in short supply. When that happens, the only thing to do is find a smaller male penguin and steal his stone.

Geese (B) and humans have at least one thing in common. They both have lasting relationships with their partners. Male geese sometimes prefer the company of other male geese, but this doesn't stop them from raising a family. The males can be joined by a female bird, and both males will look after the eggs she lays, and the tiny goslings that hatch.

The **white-fronted parrot** (C), which is native to Mexico and Central America, is believed to be the only species, other than humans, to kiss. During their courtship ritual, the two birds will lock their beaks together and gently flick their tongues. If both birds are satisfied with the kiss, the male will cement their relationship by regurgitating his food and offering it to his partner.

Female **cuckoos** (D) lay their eggs in the nests of other birds so that they don't have to look after them themselves. The foster mother will incubate the eggs and raise the offspring until they are able to fly away on their own. Curiously, each individual cuckoo mother chooses the same species to adopt all of her children and in order to ensure that her egg is not rejected, she is able to lay eggs that resemble the eggs of the foster family.

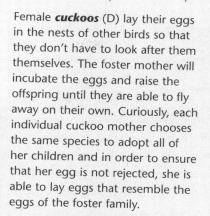

Most birds use body heat to incubate their eggs but the **Mallee fowl** (E), a member of the brush-turkey family from Australia and the Pacific Islands, keeps its eggs warm by burying them in a compost heap of rotting vegetation. As well as looking after the eggs, the male continually checks the temperature of the incubator with his beak. His aim is to ensure that the inside of the compost heap remains almost constantly at 33°C and he achieves this by adding or removing a layer of sand, when necessary. Ironically, after such care and devotion, as soon as the eggs are hatched, the parents totally ignore the chicks, which are forced to look after themselves immediately.

The home of the **Great Indian Hornbill** (F) is a prison. When the female is ready to lay her eggs, she hides in a hole in a tree. The male then seals up the hole, leaving just a narrow slit through which he passes food. Although she is unable to get out, the female has the consolation of knowing that the eggs are safe from predators such as snakes and monkeys. The female stays in there until the chicks are a few months old. She then helps the male with the feeding.

3A | Fashion statements

COMPOUND ADJECTIVES

1 Complete the missing parts of the compound adjectives.

He's (1) middle-a_____, but looks younger and is extremely (2) easy-g_____. Some days he's (3) clean-s_____ and other days he looks as if he's growing a beard. He wears comfortable, casual clothes. I think quite a few of them may be (4) second-h_____. He's particularly fond of his (5) worn-o_____ jeans, and although he's (6) well-o_____ and could afford to buy himself a whole new wardrobe, he really doesn't care.

2 Match a word from each box to form six compound adjectives.

anti	knee	middle	never	old	short

class	ending	establishment	fashioned
lived	length		

3 Complete the sentences with the compound adjectives in exercise 2.

1 Many teenage fashions claim to be rebellious and _____.

2 I remember when _____ skirts were considered incredibly boring, only to be worn as part of a school uniform.

3 Fashions in clothes and music just keep going round in _____ circles, constantly reworked and repeated.

4 Nothing is more _____ than this year's latest fashion fad. It'll have been completely forgotten in six months' time.

5 There's a thin line between being _____ and rediscovering a look from the recent past.

6 Designer fashion did not use to be for _____ women, but more people can afford it now.

VOCABULARY FROM THE LESSON

4 Complete the descriptions with the words in the box.

ethnic	flared	make-up	patterns	provocative
ripped	safety pins	velvet	wide-collared	

Tribal uniforms

The Ted
Long, knee-length
(1)_____ jackets,
straight waistcoats and
(2)_____ shirts

The Hippy
(3)_____, Indian-inspired jewellery,
(4)_____ denim jeans,
loose tops with flowery or
psychedelic (5)_____

The Punk
(6)_____, scruffy
clothes, T-shirts with
(7)_____ slogans
and studs or
(8)_____ as jewellery

The Goth
Black, nineteenth-century
style clothes and dark
(9)_____

TRANSLATION

5 Translate the text into your language.

Skateboarding has grown in popularity as an expression of youth culture over the last 30 years. Initially it was associated very closely with surfing culture, but nowadays skateboarding has its own stereotypes, music and fashions. The traditional skateboarding look is one of over-sized jeans and big, loose T-shirts, but recently skaters are tending more towards much tighter trousers and skin-tight T-shirts.

3B | The right look

EXPRESSIONS WITH *LOOK*

1 Complete the sentences with a word in the box.

| best | exchanged | feminine | got | have |
| sophisticated | through | | | |

1 Judging from the looks we _____, I think we might have been a bit overdressed.

2 She was looking her very _____, but it still wasn't good enough.

3 I looked _____ the catalogue over and over but I still couldn't find anything suitable.

4 As he got up to speak, the two girls _____ looks and burst out laughing.

5 I'm trying to go for a _____ look, something stylish and classy.

6 Did you _____ a look at that new shirt I got for you? What did you think?

7 It's nice, but it's a bit _____-looking for a guy, though. Don't you think?

2 Complete the sentences 1–6 with the phrases a–f.

A
1 I could tell by the look on his face
2 Even as she grew older,
3 I took one look at him
4 Brian looked as
5 I was furious, he had made me look
6 It's not a good idea to travel without insurance – look

B
☐ a she never lost her looks.
☐ b if he was going to cry.
☐ c what happened to Bill!
☐ d that he wasn't happy.
☐ e a complete idiot!
☐ f and decided I didn't like him.

3 Match the examples of *look* in the sentences in exercise 2 with the uses.

> **look 1** /lʊk/ verb ★★★
> 1 direct your eyes towards someone or something/ used to draw somebody's attention _____
> 2 have an appearance/seem to be _____
> **look 2** /lʊk/ noun ★★★
> 1 act of looking at somebody _____
> 2 expression on face/in eyes _____
> 3 appearance/style _____

DEFINING & NON-DEFINING RELATIVE CLAUSES

4 Circle all the possible options for each sentence.

1 It's difficult to know what to wear when you're meeting someone *which / who / that* you've never met before.
2 The best thing to do is opt for something neutral, *which / who / that* is usually easy enough.
3 The most important thing is to choose something *which / who / that* you feel comfortable in.
4 You may want to wear something brand new, *which / who / that* you've bought especially for the occasion.
5 It depends very much on the nature of the meeting and the person *which / who / that* you're going to meet.
6 Remember, what you say and what you do are far more important than the clothes *which / who / that* you choose to wear.

5 Decide which of the relative pronouns in *italics* can be omitted.

They invited us round for dinner, (1) *which* was nice. Sue cooked a special Greek dish (2) *that* she'd had on holiday. It was delicious, with fresh vine leaves (3) *that* she'd managed to buy at the local market. Her sister was there too, the one (4) *who* has just come back from the States. She was looking very glamorous in a little black cocktail dress (5) *that* she'd picked up in New York. It was covered in tiny little sequins (6) *that* glowed in the candlelight. John couldn't take his eyes off her all night!

💿 DICTATION

6 💿 **07** Write the sentences that you hear.

1 _____.

2 _____.

3 _____.

4 _____.

3c | Mirror images

PARTICIPLE CLAUSES

1 Rewrite the participle clauses in bold as full relative clauses.

Take a look at any portrait (1) **depicting a young woman** from any time in history and you will quickly understand the principles of beauty (2) **held to be universal** in that age. For example, take a look at Goya's reclining woman, 'Maya', whether (3) **dressed or undressed**, and you will understand that curves and a full figure, (4) **now considered unattractive,** were the standard of beauty at the time. Compare her to today's supermodels and underfed film stars, (5) **starving themselves to death** in order to conform to the 21st century's idea of female beauty. You don't even need to look back as far as the 19th century. Any photo of Marilyn Monroe or Sophia Loren, (6) **either posing for photographers or starring in the Hollywood blockbusters of the time**, show the same voluptuous concept of the ideal woman.

2 Rewrite the relative clauses in italics as participle clauses.

1 People *who live and work in modern cities* have no time to eat properly.
2 Young girls *who are growing up in today's consumer society* are bombarded by images of the 'perfect body'.
3 Actors or actresses *who are paid to represent beauty products* should be held responsible for the images they promote.
4 Even magazines *that claim to cover serious news stories* often feature images of celebrities.
5 Hollywood blockbusters, *which are seen by millions of cinema-goers all over the world*, invariably choose slim women in their star roles.
6 It is very difficult to control images *which are made available on the internet*.

VOCABULARY FROM THE LESSON

3 Complete the text with the words in the box.

blemish	cloud	eating	set
spotlight	susceptible		

Incomprehensible as it may be to their fans, the rich, famous and beautiful are just as (1) _____ to **self-doubt** as anyone else. No matter how **stunning** they are, the constant attention and media coverage often

(2) _____ their judgment. Every **pimple** and spot is seen as a major (3) _____ and any departure from the media-dictated norms of beauty is seen as **abnormal**. Many stars have been in the (4) _____ since **puberty,** whether on a Hollywood film (5) _____ or on the front pages of gossip magazines. So it comes as no surprise to hear that many of these celebrities suffer from serious (6) _____ disorders.

4 Complete the dictionary extracts with the words in bold in exercise 3.

1 _____ adj * not usual or typical, especially in a way that is worrying or shows that there may be something wrong or harmful

2 _____ adj impossible to understand

3 _____ noun [C] a small red lump on your skin, especially your face

4 _____ noun [U] the period in adult life when a child changes physically into an adult

5 _____ noun [U] the feeling of not having confidence in your abilities

6 _____ adj * extremely attractive

DICTATION

5 🔊 **08** Write the text that you hear.

_____

_____

_____

_____

_____

_____

_____

Naomi Wolf

3D | Model behaviour

SLANG

1 Match the words in the box to their definitions 1–8.

> an airhead   beat   blow   a drag   dumb
> a grand   nuts   psyched up

1 crazy _____

2 stupid _____

3 very tired _____

4 something or someone that is boring or causes small annoying problems _____

5 a thousand pounds or dollars _____

6 extremely excited or nervous _____

7 a silly or stupid person _____

8 to spend a lot of money quickly on things that you do not need _____

"What's that funny look for? You think my girlfriend's an airhead, don't you?"

2 Complete the sentences with words from exercise 1.

1 We'd been working all night and I was _____!

2 Yeah, can you believe it, he's won the lottery and he's going to _____ it all on a car!

3 So are you all _____ for the competition this afternoon?

4 I hate filling in all these forms, it's such _____.

5 She's just so dizzy and distracted – a complete _____.

6 I can't believe you just did that. I mean, it's just so _____!

7 He's just totally _____ about her – completely head over heels in love.

8 Yeah, it was pretty expensive, cost us more than ten _____ in the end.

ADDITION

3 Put the lines in the correct order.

☐ all of that – you get paid loads and loads of money! What could be better?

☐ you also get to stay in superb five star hotels where the welcome is just great! What's

☐ as working with some of the world's most famous photographers. And on top of

☑ I absolutely love it. I mean, besides

☐ more, you get to meet all these really interesting people as well

☐ getting the chance to travel to all these fantastic places,

TRANSLATION

4 Translate the extract from a magazine index into your language.

78 SUMMER ACCESSORIES
you can't afford to be without

HEALTH AND BEAUTY

83 PREGNANCY –
the importance of staying proud of your body

87 CHOOSING A PLASTIC SURGEON –
ten questions you should ask before going any further

94 HOW TO FIND THE RIGHT BODY SIZE FOR YOU –
and feel good about it!

96 NEW BEAUTY PRODUCTS –
we've tested all the latest from the high street shelves

97 GET A TAN –
take advantage of our special offer and get 10% off a range of sunbeds and super winter tan creams.

3 | Reading

1 Look at the dictionary entry. How do you say *lookalike* in your language?

> **lookalike** /ˈlʊkəlaɪk/ noun [C] someone who is very similar in appearance to another person, especially a famous person: *a Tom Cruise lookalike*

2 Read the interview with a celebrity lookalike and match the questions a–e to the answers.

☐ a Have you got any plans for a change of career?
☐ b How long have you been doing it?
☐ c Are all lookalikes professional actors?
☐ d So, how did you get started?
☐ e And what kind of work do you do most?

3 Choose the correct sentence ending, a, b or c.

1 Suzi Marsend
   a) looks identical to Marilyn Monroe.
   b) doesn't really sound like Marilyn Monroe.
   c) is a big fan of Marilyn Monroe.

2 She was discovered by a lookalikes agency
   a) at a fancy dress party.
   b) in a karaoke pub.
   c) at an audition.

3 She has always wanted to
   a) be a Marilyn Monroe lookalike.
   b) be an actress.
   c) run a lookalikes agency.

4 Elvis is
   a) better known than Marilyn Monroe.
   b) one of the most requested lookalikes.
   c) Suzi Marsend's favourite singer.

5 Suzi and a friend
   a) have just set up a lookalikes agency.
   b) aren't sure if they want to open a lookalikes agency.
   c) are planning to open a lookalikes agency.

4 Complete the summary with the words in bold in the interview.

How to be a celebrity lookalike

The usual route to becoming a lookalike is to send in a portfolio of photos to a lookalike agency. If they like the look of you they'll (1) _____ with you for (2) _____. You can turn up (3) _____ if you want or you can surprise them as you transform into your celebrity double in front of their very eyes. Always pay attention to detail. Invest in a professional (4) _____ and make-up and make sure you do your homework. Study photos and videos of your chosen celebrity. Concentrate on their (5) _____ and (6) _____, the way they move, the way they talk. These are the details that'll get you the job. But remember, depending on who you (7) _____ for, it can be incredibly (8) _____, so if at first you don't succeed, just keep trying. You'll get there in the end.

🔊 READ & LISTEN

5 🔊 **09** Listen to Reading 3 *How to be a celebrity lookalike* on the CD and read the article again.

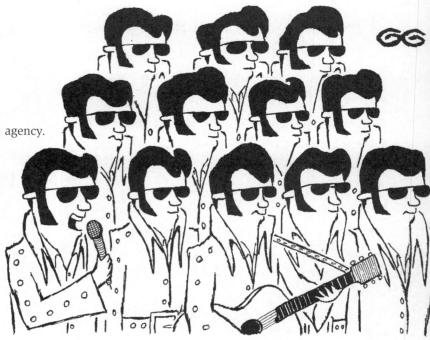

TWELVIS

Suzi Marsend is small, petite, her dark hair cut in a short, boyish style. Dressed in jeans and a T-shirt, I'm finding it hard to imagine her as Marilyn Monroe. But she spends up to six days a week playing her double. I asked her about her job and her plans for the future.

How to be a …
celebrity lookalike

1 _____

Well, it all started as a joke, really. Me and some friends, we went to this fancy dress party and I went as Marilyn, with a cheap **wig** and a second-hand dress. I don't think I looked particularly convincing, but then there was this karaoke bit in the party and everybody had to get up and do something **in character**. And I sang *Happy Birthday Mr President* – you know the one – and quite a few people commented on how I sounded just like her – and well, I really enjoyed the party but I thought nothing more of it. Till about three weeks later a lookalikes agency managed to **get in touch** with me. Apparently someone from the agency had been at the party and they wanted me to go for **an audition** … it all started from there, really.

2 _____

Off and on for about five years now. It isn't really what I dreamed about doing at drama school, but, hey, it pays the bills and it's actually a lot of fun. And it is acting too. I don't really think I look that much like Marilyn. The make-up and the professional wigs and the costumes all help obviously, but it's the **mannerisms,** the body language, the **facial expressions,** the voice, that are really important. That's what really makes a lookalike a successful lookalike. And I love all that. The acting, getting it right. At the end of the day, that's what I am, an actress playing a part, but I get a kick out of seeing myself dressed up as Marilyn too. I was never a fan of hers before, but now I am. I've seen so many of her movies so

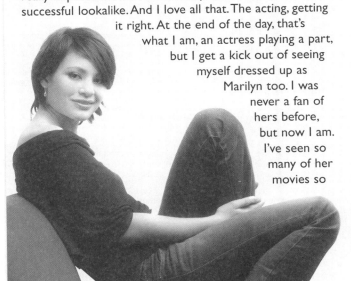

many times! She was a very talented lady.

3 _____

No, not at all. Some do just look incredibly like the celebrity they **double up** for. And that can work really well for photo shoots, you know, adverts, posters, that kind of thing, but they don't usually do quite as well if they have to actually perform. You know, sing, dance, do an interview or whatever.

4 _____

Well, all sorts. I've done stuff from TV ads to wedding parties! I've even done cameos on film sets. Most of the time it's tribute acts, you know, with other lookalikes too. I mostly do stuff alongside Elvis lookalikes. I think Marilyn and Elvis are probably the two most popular lookalikes for most events. And I just love singing along to those Elvis tunes! I do other people too, Madonna, Alanis Morrisette, Kylie Minogue, Britney Spears. I've got my own one-woman show, *Blondes Have More Fun,* which I usually tour with for a couple of weeks in the summer.

5 _____

Well, a friend and I have been talking about setting up our own lookalikes agency. It's amazing how much work there is out there for lookalikes, but it's a very **competitive** world and there are a lot of agencies too. I don't know, we're thinking about it but we haven't quite plucked up the courage to go it on our own yet. We'll see!

4A | Living in fear

WORD BUILDING

1 Complete the adjectives 1–8 with a suffix in the box.

-ful	-less	-able	-ing	-y

1 distress _____   5 reason _____

2 fear _____   6 relax _____

3 harm _____   7 risk _____

4 pain _____   8 success _____

2 Complete the text with an appropriate form of the words in brackets.

Why is it that some people are born completely
(1) _____ (*fear*) while others are born with a
completely (2) _____ (*reason*) fear of almost
everything? In actual fact, most of our (3) _____
(*anxious*) about the world around us are learnt when we
are very young. Our parents teach us to be (4) _____
(*caution*) about the dangers we face, and we learn from
experience that some things are (5) _____ (*pain*) and
some are not. But the (6) _____ (*possible*) remains
that some of us may be more genetically prone to fear than
others.

EXPLAINING REASONS

3 Complete the sentences 1–8 with the phrases a–h.

A

1 James always tried to make sure that his office could
  contact him. Otherwise,
2 He bought an expensive mobile phone in order to
3 It was important that people could contact him in case
4 He chose one with a solar battery so that
5 It was a waterproof model so that
6 He carried it with him at all times in case
7 He slept next to his phone. Otherwise,
8 He put the volume on 'extra loud' in order to

B

☐ a be online all the time.
☐ b be sure of hearing it.
☐ c he could take it in the shower.
☐ d he never ran out of power.
☐ e he suffered from terrible anxiety.
☐ f he was afraid of not hearing it.
☐ g it rang.
☐ h there was an emergency.

4 Complete the sentences.

1 He's wearing a mask. Otherwise, _____.

2 He's wearing a mask in order to _____.

3 He's wearing a mask so that _____.

4 He's wearing a mask in case _____.

DICTATION

5 🔊 **10** Write the sentences that you hear.

1 _____.

2 _____?

3 _____.

4 _____.

5 _____.

6 _____.

4B | Gladiators

PRESENT PERFECT & PAST SIMPLE

1 Change the verbs in *italics* to present perfect, where necessary.

Rome *is* one of Europe's oldest cities but it *isn't* always the capital of Italy – since Rome *is* only an official part of Italy since 1870. The city *changes* a lot in recent years. It *has* the fastest-growing economy of any Italian city and its population of two and a half million *includes* many immigrants. Rome always *attracts* people from outside the city, and, by tradition, a 'true' Roman family *lives* there for more than seven generations.

2 Put the verbs in brackets into the past simple or the present perfect.

A: (1) _____ (*you ever go*) to Rome?

B: Yes, I (2) _____ (*just come*) back actually.

A: (3) _____ (*it be*) your first visit?

B: No, I (4) _____ (*go*) loads of times. Why?

A: Well, you know I (5) _____ (*go*) there last month. I (6) _____ (*meet*) someone and I think we (7) _____ (*fall*) in love.

B: (8) _____ (*it be*) love at first sight?

A: Almost. We (9)_____ (*be*) on the phone every day since I (10) _____ (*get*) back.

B: Great news. (11) _____ (*you tell*) anyone else?

A: Yes, and they (12) _____ (*laugh*) when I (13) _____ (*say*) that we (14) _____ (*meet*) on a gladiator's course.

VOCABULARY FROM THE LESSON

3 Complete the words with the letters in the box.

a	b	d	d	e	f	m	m
n	r	s	s	u	v	v	

1 _ s s e _ t i _ e

2 _ o s _ y

3 c o n _ i _ e n t

4 d o _ i _ e e r i n g

5 r e _ e r _ e d

6 s _ l f - a s s _ r e _

7 t i _ i d

TRANSLATION

4 Translate the text into your language.

If something dramatic has ever happened to you, how did you react? If you kept a stiff upper lip at the time, the chances are that you have already forgotten quite a lot about it. This may or may not be a good thing, all depending on exactly what it was that happened to you. Some things are best forgotten.

4c | The land of the brave

WORD CLASS

1 Put the words into three groups: nouns, verbs and adjectives. Two of the words can be two different parts of speech.

> abolish   abolition   disobedience   disobedient
> disobey   free   freedom   liberate   liberation
> liberty   move   movement   rebellion   rebellious
> religion   religious

2 Find and correct four mistakes in the sentences.

> ### It happened on....
>
> **February 11th 1990** South Africa's first black president, Nelson Mandela, tastes liberate for the first time in 27 years.
>
> **May 6th 1862** Henry David Thoreau, American author of the essay 'Civil Disobedience', dies of tuberculosis.
>
> **May 12th 1916** James Connolly, leader of the failed rebel against the British, is executed in a Dublin gaol.
>
> **October 15th 1969** Millions of Americans take part in demonstrations organized by the anti-war movement, calling for an end to the fighting in Vietnam.
>
> **November 1st 1998** The European Convention on Human Rights requires all members of the EU to abolish the death penalty.
>
> **December 10th 1948** The United Nations Universal Declaration of Human Rights declares that all people have free of thought, conscience and religious.

VOCABULARY FROM THE LESSON

3 Complete the headlines with a word from the box.

> backs   boycott   granted   mass
> overturned   racial   regains   spark

1
> **Football hooligans _____ fighting across the city**

2
> **Ghana _____ independence from Britain**

3
> **Protestors call for _____ of trade talks**

4
> **Anti-terror law _____**

5
> **_____ resignation of 20 European Commissioners**

6
> **Government _____ new technology**

7
> **Fifty prisoners to be _____ freedom next week**

8
> **Police given new powers to fight _____ crimes**

DICTATION

4 🔘 **11** Write the text that you hear.

_____

_____

_____

_____

_____

_____

_____

_____

4D | Southern snakes

PRESENT PERFECT SIMPLE & CONTINUOUS

1 Three verb forms in italics are *not* possible. Find and delete them.

Snake-charming has (1) *been / been being* illegal in India since 1972. Audiences have also (2) *got / been getting* smaller because people are less afraid of snakes these days. As a result, many snake-charmers have (3) *found / been finding* it very difficult to survive. Millions have (4) *left / been leaving* the profession. Others have (5) *tried / been trying* to persuade the government to change the law. The government has (6) *agreed / been agreeing* that something needs to be done to help these people. It has (7) *looked / been looking* at ways of educating the charmers. But for many charmers, the government's ideas have (8) *come / been coming* too late.

2 Use the verbs in brackets to complete the sentences. In each sentence, use both the present perfect simple and the present perfect continuous.

1 For the last few weeks, I _____ a book about genetics, and I _____ about 75 pages. (*read*)

2 We _____ over $200 and we _____ for only two weeks. (*save*)

3 She _____ since she was very young, and she _____ more than 5 million kilometres. (*drive*)

4 He _____ his job for over ten years, but he _____ a few problems recently. (*have*)

5 The students _____ their exams this week, but they won't get the results until the teachers _____ the marking. (*do*)

3 Put the verbs in brackets into the present perfect simple or present perfect continuous. (Sometimes, both forms are possible.)

For the last nine months, Larry Thomas (1) _____ (*prepare*) for a rodeo in Oklahoma that takes place next month. He (2) _____ (*do*) three separate training courses, each of which lasted two weeks. He (3) _____ (*follow*) a special diet to build up his leg muscles and he (4) _____ (*buy*) a pair of rodeo boots for $8,000. Larry (5) _____ (*look*) forward to the event so much that he (6) _____ (*spend*) over $50,000 to get everything ready. He (7) _____ (*study*) videos of top riders and he (8) _____ (*practise*) on a mechanical training machine. Larry (9) _____ (*leave*) nothing to chance in the lead-up to the big event.

TRANSLATION

4 Translate the text into your language.

A British schoolboy has had the shock of his life after a visit to the lavatory. As the eleven-year-old lifted the seat, he was horrified to see a snake raising its head out of the water. The snake, which has still not been caught, is believed to be an American corn snake, which is not dangerous.

4 | Reading

1 Find an example of the words 1–4 in the pictures A–C on page 27 and complete the labels a–d.

1

> **framework** /ˈfreɪmwɜːk/ noun [C] ★★
> **2** a structure that supports something and makes it a particular shape: *The building had a brick base and a metal framework.*

2

> **hot-air balloon** /ˈhɒt ˈeəbəˈluːn/ noun [C] an extremely large bag full of hot air, with a basket attached that people can ride through the air in

3

> **rudder** /ˈrʌdə/ noun [C] a flat piece of wood or other material at the back of a boat or plane that is moved to change the direction of travel

4

> **wing** /wɪŋ/ noun [C] ★★★
> **1** one of the parts on a bird, insect or bat that move up and down and allow it to fly. Birds have two wings, but insects have either two or four wings.
> **2** one of the long flat parts on both sides of a plane that allow it to fly

© Mike Baldwin / Cornered

www.CartoonStock.com

"Of course it's safe.
Even has an airbag."

2 Read the article again. Answer the questions with the name of the aviator A–D.

(A: the Marquis de Bacqueville, B: Jacques Charles, C: Vincent de Groof, D: Monsieur Goupil)

Which early aviator
1 built a machine that has possibly never been tested?
2 crashed into a boat?
3 died?
4 had to pedal very fast in order to take off?
5 left his home country to make his attempt?
6 lost one machine but found success in another?
7 used a balloon to lift his machine into the air?
8 was almost too scared to make his attempt?
9 was observed by a large crowd of people?

3 Organize the words and phrases from the stories into three groups of meaning.

> coming down   connecting   descent   device
> fitted to   flying machine   invention
> landing   linked to

4 In what ways would your life be different if planes had not been invented?

🔘 READ & LISTEN

5 🔘 **12** Listen to Reading 4 *Flying Lessons* on the CD and read the article again.

Flying lessons

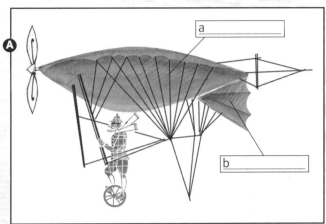

a

b

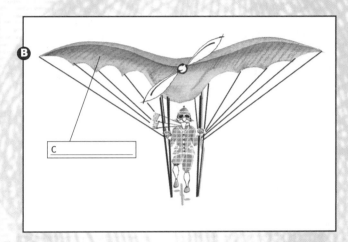

c

One of the most courageous birdmen was 62-year-old French nobleman, the Marquis de Bacqueville, who, in 1742, prepared to fly across the River Seine in Paris with paddles fitted to his arms and legs. At the last moment, he had second thoughts about his invention and asked a servant to try it out first. The servant, sensing that refusal would mean unemployment, diplomatically pointed out that a valet could not possibly precede his master. The Marquis did not know how to reply and, with a big crowd waiting below, realized he had no choice. He would have to do it himself. He jumped out of a window on the top floor of his house and began flapping his paddles vigorously. He fell to the ground like a stone, narrowly missing the pavement, but landing instead on a pile of old clothes in a washerwoman's boat. The washerwoman had stopped her boat on the riverbank in order to enjoy the spectacle. The clothes cushioned the Marquis's fall and he suffered nothing more than a broken leg.

On 27 August 1783, Jacques Alexandre César Charles released a 3.6m diameter unmanned balloon from Champ-de-Mars, Paris. It made a 45-minute flight to Gonesse but, on landing, it was attacked and destroyed by violent villagers who thought it was a monster. Their fears were reinforced by a curious smell coming from a hole in the balloon. Three months later, Charles and his friend, Nicolas Robert, lifted off from The Tuileries in Paris in a hydrogen-filled balloon. Coming down safely in a town over forty kilometres away, Charles and Robert joined the Montgolfier brothers as the world's first aviators.

Few flying machines were as bizarre as the invention of Belgian shoemaker, Vincent de Groof. His equipment – 'a device with bat-like wings'– was part flapper, part parachute. The framework was made of wood and the 12m wings were covered with waterproof silk, and controlled by three wooden levers worked by the arms and legs. The tail, also covered with strong silk, was 6m long. On 9 July 1874, de Groof planned a flight over London. He was to be taken to an altitude of 300m by balloon and then released. The ascent went well; the descent was less successful. Released over the Thames, de Groof and his machine crashed into a street in Chelsea when the wing frame failed. De Groof was killed.

The 1870s also saw Monsieur A. Goupil's aerial velocipede. The Frenchman's machine resembled a unicycle under a zeppelin. The balloon-type structure was made of wood, covered with silk, and weighed 100kg. The aeronaut stood on the pedals of the unicycle, which was linked to the balloon by connecting rods. From this position, he operated the pedals and a rudder. A description of M. Goupil's invention in the *Chronique Industrielle* explained: 'As the machine's speed increases, its weight decreases, as a result of the increase in the vertical reaction of the current. It should then ascend and remain in the air.' It is not known whether Monsieur Goupil's aerial velocipede ever passed its first test.

d

5A | Performance art

NARRATIVE TENSES

1 Find and delete eight words which should not be in the text.

The art files

Staff at FBI Headquarters in Washington DC had never given much thought to art. But, with the realization that the country was been losing as much as $2 billion each year, the FBI did set up the Art Crime Team in 2004. Twelve special agents were joined the team after they had been received special training in art crime. The agents had began to track down a long list of missing art works. By the end of their first year of operations, they had being recovered items worth over $50 million. These were included a self-portrait by Rembrandt which did had been stolen from the National Museum in Stockholm.

2 Put the verbs in brackets into the past simple, the past continuous or the past perfect.

Rembrandt (1) _____ (*live*) in modest accommodation in Amsterdam when this self-portrait (2) _____ (*be*) painted. He (3) _____ (*have*) to sell his family house and his financial problems (4) _____ (*grow*). He (5) _____ (*be*) bankrupt because he (6) _____ (*spend*) too much on his collection of old prints. Four of his children (7) _____ (*already die*) and, at 53 years of age, Rembrandt's own health (8) _____ (*begin*) to fail, although he (9) _____ (*live*) for another ten years.

ART

3 Find 13 words connected with art in the word search.

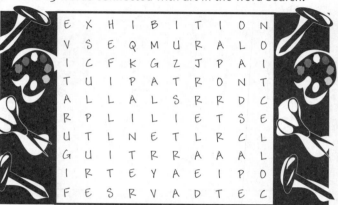

E	X	H	I	B	I	T	I	O	N
V	S	E	Q	M	U	R	A	L	O
I	C	F	K	G	Z	J	P	A	I
T	U	I	P	A	T	R	O	N	T
A	L	L	A	L	S	R	R	D	C
R	P	L	I	L	I	E	T	S	E
U	T	L	N	E	T	L	R	C	L
G	U	I	T	R	R	A	A	A	L
I	R	T	E	Y	A	E	I	P	O
F	E	S	R	V	A	D	T	E	C

4 Complete the sentences with a word from the word search in exercise 3.

1 The world's most hard-working _____ was probably Picasso, who produced hundreds of thousands of paintings, prints, illustrations and other work.

2 The world's most valuable _____ of private art is probably the J Paul Getty Museum in Los Angeles.

3 The world's largest _____, made of steel and plastic by Anish Kapoor, is 150 metres long.

4 The world's most famous _____ painter is probably Diego Rivera, whose work can be seen on the walls of the Detroit Institute of Arts.

5 The world's most expensive _____, a picture of a woman by Gustav Klimt, cost over $130 million.

6 In the world's biggest art theft, $500 million worth of paintings were stolen from a _____ in Holland.

7 The world's highest price paid for a _____ was $60 million for some fruit, a curtain and a jug by Cézanne.

DICTATION

5 🔘 **13** Write the text that you hear.

_____

_____

_____

_____

_____

5B | Priceless!

-EVER WORDS

1 Complete the sentences with a phrase in the box. More than one answer is possible.

did that	happens	he was
you are	you do	you say

1 Wherever _____, he certainly wasn't here.

2 Whatever _____, don't do that!

3 Whatever _____, this must remain a secret between us.

4 Whatever _____ is fine with me.

5 Whoever _____ is going to regret it soon.

6 Whoever _____, come out of there with your hands up.

2 Complete the sentences with *however, whatever, whenever, wherever* or *whoever*.

1 _____ much that costs, I want to buy it.

2 _____ told you that needs their head examining.

3 You can have _____ colour you like.

4 Put it _____ you want, but not in this room, please.

5 _____ you look at me like that, I know you're going to say something.

6 I'll be happy with _____ you want, my dear.

7 _____ I am, I'm always thinking of you.

EVALUATING

3 Complete the dialogues with the words in the box.

fortune	masterpiece	priceless	redeeming
rubbish	valuable	worth	worthless

- It says here that this is probably his (1)_____.
- Really? It must be worth a (2)_____.
- Yes, absolutely (3)_____, I should think. Even his early works are extremely (4)_____.
- Really? Not my kind of thing really.

THEY BOTH BITTERLY REGRETTED LYING TO THE DATING AGENCY ABOUT AN INTEREST IN ART.

MIKE TURNER

www.CartoonStock.com

- What a load of (5)_____!
- Yeah. Just a couple of lines and a badly-drawn bird. No (6)_____ features at all.
- It's amazing that people buy this stuff. It's absolutely (7)_____.
- Yes. It says $35,000, but it's (8)_____ nothing.

TRANSLATION

4 Translate the two dialogues in exercise 3 into your language.

5c | A good read

PAST PERFECT CONTINUOUS

1 Rearrange the words to make sentences.

1 been had her husband other seeing women.

_____

2 at been had she sleeping the time.

_____

3 been for had hours in she standing sun the.

_____

4 about ages been for had it she thinking.

_____

5 been for four had she trying years.

_____

6 been crowd for growing had hours the.

_____

7 been children dinner eating the front had in of the their TV.

_____

2 Match the sentences a–g to the sentences in exercise 1.

☐ a Helen decided to take early retirement.
☐ b It was no surprise that she fainted.
☐ c Mandy had to face the awful truth.
☐ d She heard absolutely nothing.
☐ e The atmosphere was electric.
☐ f There were stains all over the sofa.
☐ g She was delighted to learn that she was finally pregnant.

3 Put the verbs in brackets into the past perfect simple or continuous. Use the past perfect simple a maximum of four times.

Arundhati Roy, the Indian writer and political activist, (1) _____ (*only just turn*) 35 when she won the Man Booker prize for her first novel, *The God of Small Things*. Prior to this international success, Roy (2) _____ (*write*) movie scripts. Her work in the movie industry (3)_____ (*start*) when she was in her early 20s. She (4) _____ (*cycle*) down the street one day when she was spotted by the film director, Pradeep Krishen. In India, she (5) _____ (*become*) reasonably well-known for her TV and cinema work by the time she was about 30. Then, in the early 1990s, she found herself in court after publishing a film review in which she (6) _____ (*criticize*) a popular film about the 'Bandit Queen', Phoolan Devi. Roy decided to move out of the public eye. Four years later, she reappeared. During this time, Roy (7) _____ (*work*) on her first – and last – novel. With the fame that she (8) _____ (*win*) with the prize-winning book, Roy decided to abandon fiction and the cinema. She devoted her life to political and environmental causes. In January 2000, she was arrested in the Narmada Valley, where she (9) _____ (*protest*) against the building of a dam.

WINNER OF THE 1997 BOOKER PRIZE

The God *of* Small Things

ARUNDHATI ROY

'A masterpiece, utterly exceptional in every way'
HARPERS & QUEEN

DICTATION

4 14 Write the text that you hear.

_____

_____

_____

_____

_____

_____

_____

_____

_____

5D | Bookworm

PHRASAL VERBS 1

1 Complete the sentences 1–6 with the phrases a–f.

A
1 I don't know how she comes up with
2 It's not easy living up to
3 People really take to
4 The publishers turned down
5 With the money from her fifth book, she set up
6 She moved out of the city to bring up

B
☐ a a charitable foundation.
☐ b her children.
☐ c her first attempt to write a novel.
☐ d her reputation.
☐ e so many original ideas.
☐ f the characters in her novels.

2 Replace the phrases a–f in exercise 1 with a pronoun (*it* or *them*) and rewrite the complete sentences.

VOCABULARY FROM THE LESSON

3 Choose the best word a–c to complete the sentences.

1 She dared to _____ up at him one final time before fainting into his arms.

   (a) dangle   (b) falter   (c) glance

2 They don't come any better than this. A real _____ that will keep you turning the pages all night.

   (a) classic   (b) network   (c) regime

3 It is understood that the offenders will be kept in a _____ centre until they appear before the judge.

   (a) colossal   (b) detention   (c) pretentious

4 The panel of judges will select six entrants for the _____ list, before choosing the final winner next month.

   (a) short   (b) slot   (c) sting

5 A tireless campaigner for women's rights, she has _____ thousands of women with her TV broadcasts and best-selling books.

   (a) inspired   (b) nominated   (c) suspended

6 I don't know what we'd have done without her. She was an absolute _____, almost like an unpaid maid.

   (a) clove   (b) god-send   (c) jug

7 Brighten up your hallway with this period-style gold umbrella-holder. _____ one now while stocks last.

   (a) grab   (b) nosedive   (c) pierce

4 Match the sentences 1–7 in exercise 3 to the text types a–g.

☐ a a biography   ☐ e a romantic novel
☐ b a book review   ☐ f an advertisement
☐ c a news item   ☐ g competition rules
☐ d a personal letter

TRANSLATION

5 Translate the text into your language.

My mother did not tell me they were coming. Afterwards she said she did not want me to appear nervous. I was surprised, for I thought she knew me well. Strangers would think I was calm. I did not cry as a baby. Only my mother would note the tightness along my jaw, the widening of my already wide eyes.

(Girl with a Pearl Earring, by Tracy Chevalier, *chapter 1)*

5 | Reading

1 Do you associate any of the words in the box with the pictures on page 33?

> defensive   difficult   impatient   introverted
> resistant   selfish   sensitive   shy

2 Read the introduction and interview answers. Match the answers A–E to the questions 1–5.

- ☐ 1 What do you enjoy doing most?
- ☐ 2 What do you find hardest in your professional life?
- ☐ 3 What do you remember most about the place where you grew up?
- ☐ 4 What do your paintings mean? Can you explain them?
- ☐ 5 Would you have plastic surgery?

3 Find evidence in the text for the statements 1–8.

1 He does not share a studio with another artist.
2 He doesn't mind if other people understand his paintings differently.
3 He hasn't always made his living as a visual artist.
4 He often spends time with potential customers.
5 He understands that not everyone wants to buy his work.
6 He's a great fan of some Asian body art.
7 He's very interested in performance art.
8 His family helped him develop his talent.

4 Read the text again and identify what the words in italics refer to.

1 I had to draw an eye and I asked *her* to help me. *She* told me a story about how *she* had had to learn to draw when *she* was a child.
2 I probably enjoy *it* more than the other things I do. I like to use my fingers. I like to be able to touch.
3 I went *there* with a girl who was also doing the course. She told me *it* was a great place to study.
4 *It* will always remind me that I'm artist, *it*'s a part of who I am.
5 *It* would have been interesting, and well-paid, too.
6 The people *there* are friendly, warm, cool, open-minded, more than over here. Maybe I'll want to go back *there* one day.

5 🔊 **15** Listen to Reading 5 *Michel Soucy* on the CD and read the text again.

Michel Soucy (Schefferville, Canada, 1963–)

Paintings

Drawings

Photography

Bio

News

Links

contact

Michel Soucy, a Canadian scenic and visual artist, who graduated from Central Saint Martin's College of Arts and Design in London, has worked in the world of the arts for about twenty-five years.

As a painter and a scenographer, his work can be seen in art galleries, museums and live performances around the world. Beginning in his native Canada, he has since lived and worked in Finland, Britain and the Netherlands.

Now living in Brussels, his work is attracting wider and wider audiences in Europe, Asia and North America.

A

I guess it must be the snow. The cold and the river. We moved to Montreal from Schefferville when I was six and everything started there. I started writing stories when I was very young and my mother, who had worked in fashion design, helped me learn to draw. After graduating from high school, I worked as an actor for ten years and, even then, my work was about communication, about what it is to communicate with another person.

B

Yes, of course. But everybody has their own meaning, and I prefer it when other people bring their own interpretations to my work. But it's all people, I mean, my paintings are always about people and they are usually, no, not usually – the people are *always* alone. And that's because we are all alone, everybody is alone. And with my painting, I have to paint alone.

C

What I really like to do is the skin, the texture of the skin. At school, I wanted to be a plastic surgeon. I wanted to recreate the human body, a sort of Dr Frankenstein. I think if I hadn't been a painter, I'd have been a performance artist like Orlan. I respect her work, she's a very refined artist. I met her once at a conference in Montreal when I did some interpreting for her.

D

No, not today. But tattoos are different. I had my first when I was about 20 – it's an artist's palette on my ankle. It was a way of saying, 'Me, I'm a painter'. It's in my skin now. Then, some time later, I had a film strip done on my shoulder. You could say that movies are inside of me also now. And, maybe, ten years later I had a Japanese fish done on my left arm. Some of the Japanese designs are fantastic.

E

If you're not signed up to one gallery, or one agent, you have to be your own salesman, your own agent, and that can be kind of hard. And, of course, what it is that you want to say in your paintings, what you want to express as a painter, isn't necessarily something that people out there want to buy. But you have to make a living. One of the reasons, I guess, why I do different things.

6A | At the polls

REAL & UNREAL CONDITIONS

1 Insert the words in brackets in the sentences.

1 Anyone can become the president of the US they want to badly enough and they're ready to work hard to get what they want. (*provided*)

2 Don't enter politics you know exactly why you're doing it and what you want out of it. (*unless*)

3 He might have won the election he hadn't lost his temper and insulted his opponent live on TV. (*if*)

4 I would only enter politics I could guarantee the privacy of my wife and children. (*so long as*)

5 I'll give up my post as governor I can run for president. (*on condition that*).

6 He would never have been so successful it hadn't been for his wife. (*if*)

7 I would never, ever consider a life in politics, of course, I was asked to. (*unless*)

8 You want a career in politics you'll have to be prepared to give up everything else, friends, family and all your free time. (*if*)

2 Which sentences in exercise 1 are real and which are unreal conditions?

3 Correct the grammatical errors in the quotations.

1 If you pick up a starving dog and make him prosperous, he did not bite you. This is the principal difference between a man and a dog. (*Mark Twain*)

2 If we couldn't laugh, we'll all go insane. (*Jimmy Buffet*)

3 There is a theory which states that if ever anybody will discover exactly what the Universe is for and why it is here, it will instantly disappear and be replaced by something even more bizarre and unexplicable. (*Douglas Adams*)

4 Americans will put up with anything provided it didn't block traffic. (*Dan Rather*)

5 Nobody would have believed in you unless you believe in yourself (*Liberace*)

6 Oh, I don't blame Congress. If I have $600 billion at my disposal, I'd be irresponsible too. (*Lichty and Wagner*)

DICTATION

4 🔊 **16** Write the sentences that you hear.

1 _____

2 _____

3 _____

4 _____

5 _____

POLL RESULTS ARE IN... 90% OF AMERICANS CAN'T SPELL SCHWARZENNEGER.

NEWS

www.CartoonStock.com

SCHWADRON

6B | Women in politics

I WISH / IF ONLY

1 Complete the sentences 1–6 with the phrases a–f.

A

1 I'm broke, homeless and divorced.
2 I'm not satisfied with your work.
3 I'm sorry I can't promise you that.
4 It's a pity I don't know any politicians.
5 Unfortunately, I never worked much at school.
6 Why did I say something so stupid?

B

- [ ] a I wish I hadn't.
- [ ] b I wish I were.
- [ ] c I wish I weren't.
- [ ] d If only I could.
- [ ] e If only I did.
- [ ] f If only I had.

2 Put the verbs in brackets in the correct form.

1 **A**: He seemed such an honest, trustworthy person.

   B: Yes. If only we _____ (know) then what we know now.

2 **A**: I'm really missing you.

   B: Me, too. I wish you _____ (be) here.

3 **A**: I told your husband everything.

   B: You know what? I really wish you _____. (not / do) that.

4 **A**: It's a beautiful view, isn't it?

   B: Yes, it is. But I wish it _____ (not / rain).

5 **A**: So, you had a good time last night?

   B: Yes! If only you _____ (be) there. You'd have loved it.

ELECTIONS

3 Complete the sentences with an appropriate word.

1 In New Zealand, there are always at least seven Maori M _ _ _ _ _ _ of Parliament.

2 In some European elections, the t _ _ _ _ _ _ has been as low as 20%.

3 Many British schools are used as p _ _ _ _ _ _ stations on election days.

4 Outer Delhi, the world's largest parliamentary c _ _ _ _ _ _ _ _ _ _ _ _, has over three million voters.

5 Over 150,000 Londoners could not understand how to fill in the b _ _ _ _ _ papers in a recent local election.

6 The American Prohibition Party (which wants to prohibit all alcohol) has nominated a c _ _ _ _ _ _ _ _ _ in every US presidential election since 1872.

7 There are still a few countries where g _ _ _ _ _ _ elections do not take place.

VOCABULARY FROM THE LESSON

5 Complete the text with the words in the box.

committed	fight	involved	represented	run
set	step	voted		

Many Hollywood stars have been (1) _____ in political action of one kind or another. Some, like Ronald Reagan, (2) _____ their sights on, and get, the top job. Others, like Clint Eastwood, are happy to (3) _____ for office in smaller jobs – Eastwood was mayor of Carmel in California for two years before deciding to (4) _____ aside, even though 72% of the electorate had (5) _____ for him. Still others, like Danny De Vito or Robert De Niro, give tens of thousands of dollars to help their political friends (6) _____ elections. The Democrats are generally better (7) _____ in Hollywood than the Republicans, but there are many, like Bruce Willis or Mel Gibson, who are (8) _____ to the Republican cause.

TRANSLATION

6 Translate the poem into your language.

> If only I could know you
> I've watched you now so long
> If only I could know your name
> And know your favorite song
>
> If only I could know you
> I see you every day
> But any time you look at me
> I turn and look away
>
> I wonder if you've noticed me
> I try hard not to stare
> But even if you've seen my face
> You'll never see I care
>
> Fred Hobbs

6c | Politically incorrect

EMBARRASSMENT

1 Put the lines in the correct order.

- ☐ ashamed, or even in some cases
- ☑ How do you usually cope with acute
- ☐ bright red? Some people are not at all self-
- ☐ humiliated at the slightest mistake.
- ☐ embarrassment? Do you laugh it off or go
- ☐ situations without even blushing. But other people squirm
- ☐ uncomfortably and feel acutely
- ☐ conscious and can brush off embarrassing

SHOULD HAVE

2 Choose the more appropriate response, a or b, to the sentences 1–6.

1 It's my birthday.
   (a) I shouldn't have told you.
   (b) You should have told us!

2 We've organized a surprise party for you.
   (a) I should have guessed!
   (b) I should have learnt by now.

3 I'm sorry. I've completely forgotten his number.
   (a) You should have written it down.
   (b) You shouldn't have bothered.

4 We've brought you a little present.
   (a) It shouldn't have happened.
   (b) Oh, you shouldn't have!

5 Come on, you dirty rat!
   (a) I should have seen it coming.
   (b) You shouldn't have said that!

6 I don't care if it was my fault.
   (a) You should have apologized.
   (b) You should have seen it.

7 Why the secret?
   (a) I'm sorry. I should have mentioned it before.
   (b) I don't know. I really shouldn't have.

8 I must speak to the bank manager later today.
   (a) Why should you have done that?
   (b) Shouldn't you have done that yesterday?

3 Read the text and write six sentences about it, which include *should have* or *shouldn't have*.

In the 1870s, the US government fought a war against the Lakota tribes whose land the government wanted to take. Breaking a treaty with the Lakota, the US forces attacked. Colonel George Custer was made leader of a cavalry division despite the fact that he had a very poor service record. During one campaign, Custer's cavalry advanced much faster than the foot-soldiers and the rest of the army. Coming across a combined force of Lakota and Cheyenne, Custer ignored his orders not to attack. He also refused to listen to the advice of his scouts. Custer was almost certainly motivated by the thought that a heroic victory would get him into the White House. Even though he knew he had fewer soldiers than the enemy, he divided his men into three groups in order to attack the village on the Little Big Horn River. The Native Americans of Chief Sitting Bull were waiting for them. None of the 210 men of the Seventh Cavalry survived. It was even worse for the Lakota. Within a year the whole tribe had been destroyed.

● DICTATION

4 ● **17** Write the text that you hear.

_____

_____

_____

_____

_____

_____

_____

_____

6D | Politically correct

-ISMS

1 Choose the best description, a or b, for each slogan 1–5.

1 (a) anti-sexist (b) sexist
2 (a) elitist (b) idealist
3 (a) racist (b) socialist
4 (a) optimist (b) pacifist
5 (a) ageist (b) realist

2 Match the words in the box to the definitions 1–6.

anarchist	atheist	capitalist
fatalist	individualist	materialist

1 someone who believes that God does not exist
   _____

2 someone who believes that there should be no
   government or laws _____

3 someone who believes that you cannot prevent things
   from happening, especially bad things _____

4 someone who believes that money and possessions are
   the most important aspects of human existence
   _____

5 someone who does things in their own way without
   worrying about what other people think or do
   _____

6 someone who is successful in business or invests
   money in business for profit _____

ASKING FOR & GIVING CLARIFICATION

3 Complete the dialogue with the words in the box.

basically	follow	know	mean	meant
point	suggesting	words		

A: It's a very serious situation, you know.

B: Yes, I know, I (1) _____. But what are you
(2) _____? That I should apologize?

A: Well, maybe it's time that you thought about doing
something else.

B: I don't (3) _____. What do you (4) _____?

A: Well, you know, look around. Consider your options.

B: I see. So, (5) _____, you're saying that I should
resign?

A: No, that's not what I (6) _____. My
(7) _____ is simply that you should seriously
consider your position.

B: In other (8) _____, resign.

A: Yes.

TRANSLATION

4 Translate the text into your language.

Good evening. This is the 37th time I have spoken to you
from this office in which so many decisions have been
made that shape the history of this nation. Each time I
have done so to discuss with you some matters that I
believe affected the national interest.

In all the decisions I have made in my public life I have
always tried to do what was best for the nation. Throughout
the long and difficult period of Watergate, I have felt it
was my duty to persevere; to make every possible effort to
complete the term of office to which you elected me.

(extract from *President Nixon's resignation speech, 1974*)

1 Which word from the dictionary extracts best describes the quotations 1–4?

> **cynical** /ˈsɪnɪkəl/ adj ★
> **1** someone who is cynical believes that people care only about themselves and are not sincere or honest

> **ironic** /aɪˈrɒnɪk/ or **ironical** /-ɪkəl/ adj **1** expressing the opposite of what you really think, especially in order to be humorous: *an ironic comment an ironic little smile*

> **satirical** /səˈtɪrɪkəl/ or **satiric** /səˈtɪrɪk/ adj satirical writing or art uses humour to criticize people or things and make them seem silly: *a satirical novel | programme | play a satirical look at politics today*

1 I never vote for anyone. I always vote against. (*WC Fields*)
2 He knows nothing, and he thinks he knows everything. That points clearly to a political career. (*GB Shaw*)
3 Men enter local politics solely as a result of being unhappily married. (*C Northcote Parkinson*)
4 Since a politician never believes what he says, he is quite surprised to be taken at his word. (*Charles de Gaulle*)

2 Read the four newspaper extracts and choose the most appropriate headlines, 1 or 2.

www.CartoonStock.com

A

1

> ## 'I made a mistake about Bell,' admits Hamilton

2

> ## BBC man Bell found not guilty

> Martin Bell, the independent anti-corruption MP who overturned a government majority of 15,000 to win the Tatton seat in the last general election, has been cleared of irregular election expenses. Former BBC journalist, Bell, had been accused of receiving payments for legal expenses during the election campaign, but the inquiry found no evidence of wrongdoing. Neil Hamilton, the former MP who lost his seat after being accused of corruption, has also been accused of failing to declare all his election expenses. Hamilton, whose political career is now in ruins, continues the fight to clear his name, but the evidence against him looks overwhelming.

B

1

> ## BRITISH MPS IN CASH-FOR-QUESTIONS SCANDAL

2

> ## MPS ARRESTED AFTER ATTACK ON BUSINESSMAN

> Two MPs from Britain's ruling party have accepted money from a businessman in exchange for asking questions on the businessman's behalf in the British parliament, according to reports in the British press. The two MPs and government ministers, Mr Neil Hamilton and Mr Tim Smith, received cash in brown envelopes as payment for helping Mr Mohamed Al-Fayed, a London-based businessman and the owner of the world-famous Harrods superstore. It is understood that Mr Smith has already admitted his guilt and will announce his resignation shortly. But with an election approaching, the other man, Mr Neil Hamilton, has denied any wrongdoing and has vowed to fight for his seat. However, the British government looks set to lose the poll and Mr Hamilton's involvement in the scandal is not helping their cause.

C

1

Al-Fayed celebrates victory over Hamilton

2

Harrods store to close

There were scenes of both jubilation and despair outside London's High Court yesterday. After five years of fighting to clear his name in the 'Cash-for-Questions' scandal, disgraced former MP, Neil Hamilton, insisted he would appeal against the judge's decision, but he now faces huge legal fees and other costs that he may not be able to meet. The jury in the packed courtroom announced that they had found Mr Hamilton guilty of accepting payments from Mohamed Al-Fayed, the owner of Harrods. Outside the court, a smiling Mr Al-Fayed told the crowd that people like Neil Hamilton should never be in power. Hamilton lost first his ministerial position and then his seat in Parliament after allegations surfaced in the press concerning money he had received from the Egyptian businessman. On a recent appearance on a satirical TV show, Hamilton received his appearance fee in cash in a brown paper bag at the end of the show. Hamilton will now need more than that to rebuild his life.

D

1

VOTERS CAN'T COUNT

2

HAMILTON LOSES COUNT TO BELL

As expected, anti-corruption candidate, Martin Bell, swept past the disgraced Neil Hamilton in the Tatton constituency. Hamilton, holding a majority of 15,000 voters from the last election, lost his seat to the victorious Bell by a huge margin of 11,000 votes.

3 Read the extracts again and put them in the order in which they were printed, so that they tell the whole story.

4 Complete the sentences with A (Neil Hamilton), B (Martin Bell), C (Mohamed Al-Fayed).

1 _____'s reputation has been ruined.

2 _____ attempted to corrupt senior politicians.

3 _____ did not get money to pay his lawyers.

4 _____ preferred to be paid in cash.

5 _____ should probably have resigned earlier.

6 _____ wanted the government to listen to him.

7 _____ was proved innocent.

8 _____ won the support of ordinary people.

5 Complete the sentences with a word from the newspaper articles.

1 Despite being one-nil down, they o_____d the score and went on to win four–one.

2 She was f_____d not guilty on all the charges that were brought against her.

3 The government was a_____d of giving inaccurate information to the public.

4 He always goes through the 'Nothing to d_____e' channel at the airport.

5 She vowed to c_____r her name fully and fast.

6 The prime minister d_____d any knowledge of the scandal.

7 The government f_____s enormous costs to repair the damage.

8 When allegations of corruption s_____d during the inquiry, he admitted them immediately.

🔘📖 READ & LISTEN

6 🔘📖 **18** Listen to Reading 6 *Cash-for-questions* on the CD and read the article again.

7A | Green issues

THE ENVIRONMENT

1 Choose the best words to complete the text.

> Have you noticed how it's getting hotter every summer? You can't tell me it's not connected with global (1) *fuels / warming*. It's all those greenhouse (2) *gases / panels* that are warming the planet. Part of the problem is that there are too many cars and the exhaust (3) *organic / fumes* are polluting everything and a few (4) *global / wind* farms or (5) *hydro-electric / solar* panels here and there aren't going to be enough to reverse the climate (6) *change / glazing*. Anyway, we've started eating organic (7) *consumption / food* in our family and we recycle everything.

VOCABULARY FROM THE LESSON

2 Combine words from each box to make compound nouns.

car	fire
chronic	organic
carrier	coastal
plant	printer

areas	illnesses
bags	ink
crops	retardants
dyes	tyres

3 Complete the sentences with a pair of words from exercise 2.

1 More and more farmers are growing _____ to meet the demand for safe food.

2 Many people who live in _____ are worried about their homes if sea levels rise.

3 Air pollution can be responsible for lung disease, asthma and other _____.

4 More than 500 billion plastic _____ are given away by shops and supermarkets every year.

5 _____ are not always safer than chemical or industrially produced ones.

6 The rubber of _____ gives off poisonous fumes when it burns.

7 Some companies sell printers very cheaply, so that you have to buy their expensive _____.

8 Some _____ that were used in the past have killed more people than they have saved.

💿 DICTATION

4 💿 **19** Write the text that you hear.

_____

_____

_____

_____

_____

_____

_____

_____

(extract from *United Nations Framework Convention on Climate Change*)

7B | Green houses

FUTURES REVIEW

1 Choose the best verb form to complete the sentences.

1 It looks like it's *being / going to be* another beautiful day today.
2 Sea levels *are rising / will rise* dramatically over the next fifty years.
3 Local governments *are meeting / will meet* to discuss plans to improve recycling systems this weekend.
4 Water consumption *is not decreasing / will not decrease* until excess water usage is made punishable by law.
5 The neighbours decided that *they're going to have / they'll have* solar panels fitted on the kitchen roof.
6 That looks heavy! Let me help. You get that end and *I'm grabbing / I'll grab* this end.

2 Change six of the verbs in italics to a more appropriate form with *going to* + infinitive, present continuous or present simple.

A: (1) *Will you fix* that tap or not? And if so, when?
B: Yes, (2) *I'll do* it soon. I promise.
A: Because my father (3) *will come* round for lunch tomorrow. (4) *I'll ask* him to bring his tools, if you like.
B: No, that's OK. (5) *I'll do* it as soon as (6) *I'll have* a spare moment.
A: And when (7) *will that be*?
B: Well, not today because (8) *I'll have* an appointment with the doctor at four.
A: But (9) *that'll only last* half an hour.
B: Yes, but after that, (10) *I'll see* Winston for a drink.
A: Oh right. And (11) *will you do* anything special tomorrow morning?
B: No, (12) *I'll probably have* a lie-in.
A: You know what? (13) *I'll get* my father to do it.

EXPRESSIONS WITH *MAKE*

3 Complete the sentences with the prepositions in the box.

for   of   to   with

1 I promise I'll make more time _____ you in the future.
2 I think I could make do _____ very little if I had to.
3 I'm sorry, but it doesn't make any sense at all _____ me.
4 It looks like make or break _____ me at work in the next few days.
5 We should always try to make the most _____ what we've got.
6 Let's make it easy _____ everyone to understand.
7 Why do you always make a point _____ being late?
8 It doesn't make any difference _____ me.

TRANSLATION

4 Translate the text into your language.

GREENPEACE

Greenpeace exists because this fragile earth deserves a voice. It needs solutions. It needs change. It needs action.

Greenpeace is a non-profit organization, with a presence in 40 countries across Europe, the Americas, Asia and the Pacific.

To maintain its independence, Greenpeace does not accept donations from governments or corporations, but relies on contributions from individual supporters and foundation grants.

7c | Lifestyle changes

FUTURE PERFECT & FUTURE CONTINUOUS

1 Insert the missing words (*be* and *have*) in sentences 1–7.

1 Heather is training to become a life coach. As soon as she's qualified, she'll looking for work.
2 But before she earns anything, she'll spent over $1000 on her training.
3 She'll having her next class at 3 o'clock on Tuesday afternoon.
4 After that, she'll done nearly two-thirds of the course.
5 She'll taking her final exam in December.
6 If she passes that, she'll starting her 'experience programme' immediately afterwards.
7 She hopes she will completed all her training by next summer.

2 Look at the diary page. Write three sentences in each of the following ways.

1 *She'll be …*
2 *She'll have …*

Week 13   **March–April**

TODAY Monday 27

11.15 – 11.45 Coaching observation
N.B. Start working on portfolio!

Tuesday 28

2.30 – 3.30 Roleplay workshop
4.30 – 6.00 Lecture: Principles of Listening

Wednesday 29

4.30 – 6.00 Lecture: Active Listening

Thursday 30

11.15 – 11.45 Coaching observation

Friday 31

3.30 – 4.30 Roleplay workshop
5.00 Hand in portfolio!

Saturday 1

8.30 Class meal (L'Oreille à la Bouche)

Sunday 2

Start work on assignment 5!!

VOCABULARY FROM THE LESSON

3 Choose the best word a–c to complete the sentences.

1 I won't say who told me, but it was a _____ friend.
   (a) blanket   (b) glove   (c) mutual

2 I'm afraid it's simply a question of will _____.
   (a) force   (b) power   (c) strength

3 He's trying to get in _____ before he goes skiing.
   (a) fit   (b) shape   (c) step

4 There's no point having plans unless you put them into _____.
   (a) action   (b) lifestyle   (c) pinpoint

5 Let's _____ up an action plan and then decide who does what.
   (a) call   (b) draw   (c) pull

6 Even if you don't _____ all your goals, it's still worth the effort.
   (a) get   (b) have   (c) reach

7 I think it's time we cleared the _____ between us.
   (a) air   (b) barrier   (c) block

8 I appreciate your _____ support, but money would also help.
   (a) approve   (b) moral   (c) supplement

🔘 DICTATION

4 🔘 **20** Write the conversation that you hear.

A: _____

B: _____

A: _____

B: _____

A: _____

B: _____

A: _____

7D | Trends

GIVING EXAMPLES

1 Put the lines in the correct order.

- ☐ as yoga or Tai Chi. But I'll make the changes gradually. I may start, for
- ☐ example, by only watching four hours of TV a day.
- ☑ I'm seeing a life coach because, among other
- ☐ instance, might be quite fun. I plan to change my diet and cut down on chips, in
- ☐ particular. We're also talking about other things I can do, such
- ☐ things, I want to lead a healthier lifestyle. I'm going to give up some of my hobbies, like
- ☐ video games, and take up a sport. Squash, for

2 Delete five expressions in italics that do not belong to the text.

If you want to find out about the future, there are many people, *among other things*, who can help you. You can turn, *for example*, to the horoscope pages of *such as* the newspaper where you can find out about your love life, *in particular*. For more serious information, you can dip into the writing of well-known prophets *such as* Nostradamus or use magical books *like* the I Ching, *to name but a few*. But if you're really serious *for instance* about the future, you can take a course, *in particular*, in Futures Studies. At the University of Budapest, *for instance*, you can study topics *like* 'Change and Future' or 'Space and Time in Futures Studies', *to name but two*.

www.CartoonStock.com

"You see me coming here every week and paying you fifty dollars ..."

NOUNS & PREPOSITIONS

3 Complete the sentences with a phrase in the box.

> A growing interest   An increase   A shortage
> Annual consumption   The British taste
> Rapid advances   The developing world's demand

1 _____ for cheap energy is set to grow and grow.

2 _____ for home improvements is reflected in many DIY programmes on TV.

3 _____ in computer technology have changed the way we live.

4 _____ in green issues will lead to more eco-holidays.

5 _____ in road taxes may be the only way to cut exhaust fumes.

6 _____ of bottled water in Italy has reached nearly 200 bottles per person.

7 _____ of fossil fuels will mean we have to find alternative energy sources.

TRANSLATION

4 Translate the quotations into your language.

1 'Everything that can be invented has been invented.' (Charles H Duell, US government official, 1899)

2 'It will be gone by June.' (*Variety* magazine, referring to rock 'n roll, 1955)

3 'Nuclear-powered vacuum cleaners will probably be a reality in 10 years.' (Alex Lewyt, president of a vacuum cleaner company, 1955)

4 'It's a great invention but who would want to use it anyway?' (US president, R B Hayes, after a demonstration of a telephone, 1876)

5 'There is no reason anyone would want a computer in their home.' (Ken Olson, computer manufacturer, 1977)

6 'It is apparent to me that the possibilities of the aeroplane, which two or three years ago were thought to hold the solution to the (flying machine) problem, have been exhausted, and that we must turn elsewhere.' (Thomas Edison, American inventor, 1895)

7 'A rocket will never be able to leave the Earth's atmosphere.' (*New York Times*, 1936)

7 | Reading

1 Match the extracts 1–5 to the types of magazine a–e.

- ☐ a food magazine
- ☐ b football magazine
- ☐ c gardening magazine
- ☐ d gossip and celebrities magazine
- ☐ e interior design magazine

1

> of the Rolling Stones. At last year's event in Dordrecht, thousands of fans turned out to line the streets as Her Royal Highness the Princess of

2

> defeat for Mourinho. In the press conference after the match, scorer of a hat-trick and captain of the champions this season, Thierry

3

> great thing about some of these new hybrids is that they'll stay in flower right through to November if they are regularly watered and taken care of. The brightest colours include a huge scarlet bloom that

4

> will be arriving in the shops soon. They have a much more delicate flavour and should be served with a small slice of lemon and a sprinkling of sea salt. A few chopped

5

> expert advice, tune in on Wednesday evenings at 9.10 for the latest tips on colour schemes, ways to brighten up your home and, of course, Laurence, with an update on his transformation

2 Look at the photo and headline on the magazine page.

1 What kind of magazine is this from?
2 Which six of the following topics do you think are mentioned?

a her favourite football team
b her physical shape
c her reasons for going to Shanghai
d her relationship with other members of the royal family
e her work
f news of her family
g the clothes she is wearing
h the people she met in Shanghai
i the things she believes in

3 Read the article to check your answer to exercise 2.

4 Read the article again and answer the questions.

1 How do we know that the streets of Shanghai were very busy on the day of Lady Helen's visit?
2 How do we know that Lady Helen does not want to publicize her royal connections?
3 How do we know that Armani's show in Shanghai was 'one of the events of the year'?
4 How do we know that Lady Helen has had health problems?
5 How do we know that Lady Helen likes her work?

5 Find a phrase in the article that tells us …

1 that Lady Helen was looking for something to buy.
2 that her royal status sometimes helps her get something she wants.
3 that her work involves a lot of travel.
4 that Lady Helen is often very hungry.
5 that she is happy to advertise for Armani.

6 Answer the question.

Do you ever read magazines like this? Why or why not?

🔘 READ & LISTEN

7 🔘 **21** Listen to Reading 7 *Lady Helen Taylor* on the CD and read the article again.

Lady Helen Taylor

Busy Mother Of Four Makes A Special Visit To Shanghai

It's Saturday morning in Shanghai and it seems that many of the city's 20 million inhabitants are out shopping. A few look curiously at the slender, blonde tourist browsing at the stalls and antiques markets in the Old Town. Most stare because of what she is – blonde and beautiful – rather than *who* she is – Lady Helen Taylor, the daughter of the Duke and Duchess of Kent, and a cousin of the Queen.

But Lady Helen has never broadcast her royal status. Although she regards her title as a privilege, and admits it would be disingenuous to claim it is not quite useful at times, she prefers to introduce herself simply as Helen Taylor.

She is far more ready to chat about her role as roving ambassador for Giorgio Armani. Helen, 41, was in Hong Kong and Shanghai for gala showings of Armani's 'Privé couture' collection – the first in China – as well as the opening of the designer's 30-year retrospective at Shanghai's Art Museum. The Shanghai gala was one of the events of the year, attracting the daughter of the president, Mrs David Mao, along with other guests such as Ziyi Zhang, star of *Memoirs of a Geisha*, and the Asian superstar Jerry Yan.

Work prevented Helen's husband, the art dealer Tim Taylor, from joining her. The couple have four children – Columbus, eleven, Cassius, nine, Eloise, three, and a baby, Estella, born fourteen months ago. Helen has already regained her size 10 figure with regular gym and Pilates sessions. And, she says: 'Armani's clothes are a very good curb on my voracious appetite.'

She is also a great believer in acupuncture, osteopathy 'for my bad back after having child number four,' and cranial osteopathy. 'When I finish a cranial osteopathy session, I feel energized; it helps to realign everything.'

Earlier this year, she signed her seventh yearly contract with Armani. 'It's a bit like being a fashion diplomat,' she says. 'I will always back the brand because I love his clothes. But on a personal level, I do it because I am increasingly fond of him. We have a lot of fun. He is so passionate about his work, he's always happy and surrounded by a great team; it's inspiring.'

8A | Cold comfort

Symptoms

1 Match the adjectives 1–6 to the nouns a–f to describe symptoms.

A		B	
1	hacking	☐ a	stomach
2	runny	☐ b	temperature
3	high	☐ c	cough
4	throbbing	☐ d	muscles
5	stiff	☐ e	nose
6	upset	☐ f	headache

2 Match the completed symptoms in exercise 1 to the advice given.

1 Get someone to give you a massage, or take a long, warm bath. _____

2 Suck a mint sweet or drink a glass of milk and honey – that should help the pain. _____

3 Eat boiled rice and fish until you feel better. _____

4 Use very soft tissue or the skin might get sore. _____

5 You may need to use a cool sponge, or take a cool shower to bring it down. _____

6 Take an aspirin and lie down in a dark room until it goes away. _____

3 Reorder the sentences to make three short dialogues.

A: At the chemist
☐ and if you're not feeling better, see a doctor.
☐ Have you got anything for a sore throat?
☐ Take one of these every four hours for two days,

B: At the doctor's
☐ OK, lie down over there and I'll have a look.
☐ What exactly seems to be the problem?
☐ I've been having these terrible pains.

C: Calling in sick
☐ I hope it's nothing serious.
☐ Take it easy and let us know if you're coming in tomorrow.
☐ I'm sorry, I don't think I'm going to make it in today.
☐ I've got an upset stomach and a bit of a temperature.

Vocabulary from the lesson

4 Complete the text using an appropriate form of the verbs in the box.

be off	take	go off
lose	sound	come across

A: Where's James?

B: He (1) _____ work today. He called earlier and he (2) _____ like death. He said he had a temperature and that he had (3) _____ his food.

A: That's not like James to (4) _____ his appetite. He usually eats like a horse! There must be something wrong with him!

B: So I told him to (5) _____ it easy and give us a call later today. I tried not to (6) _____ as being too anxious, but, well, you know …

A: Yes, I know, we've got that meeting tomorrow and we really need him to be here!

Translation

5 Translate the jokes into your language.

1 **Patient:** Doctor, Doctor, I think I need glasses.
   Doctor: You certainly do, Sir, this is a fish and chip shop!

2 **Patient:** Doctor, Doctor, I keep getting pains in the eye when I drink coffee.
   Doctor: Have you tried taking the spoon out?

3 **Patient:** Doctor, Doctor, when I press with my finger here … it hurts, and here … and here … .What do you think is wrong with me?
   Doctor: You have a broken finger!

WELL WE OBVIOUSLY HAVE TO WAIT FOR THE FULL RESULTS TO COME BACK FROM THE LAB.. BUT IF I HAD TO HAZARD A GUESS I'D SUSPECT YOU WERE A BIT UNDER THE WEATHER!

www.CartoonStock.com

8B | Bill of health

HEALTH IDIOMS

1 Rearrange the words to form sentences.

1 weather a feeling she under the bit was

_____ .

2 something think I coming down am with I

_____ .

3 round definitely going there's bug a

_____ .

4 killing back my me was

_____ .

5 given bill he clean of was health a

_____ .

6 yesterday door I at was death's thought I

_____ .

2 Complete the sentences 1–6 in exercise 1 with the phrases a–f.

☐ a which was a surprise, considering his lifestyle.
☐ b but I'm feeling much better today.
☐ c so I decided to have a massage.
☐ d so she went to bed.
☐ e there are at least five people off work this week.
☐ f so I'm going to take an aspirin.

MODALS OF SPECULATION

3 Find and correct four mistakes in the verbs in italics.

A: Where can she be? She should have been here by now.
B: I don't know. Anything *must have happened* to her.
A: She *can have got* lost.
B: No, I gave her a map.
A: Well, she *may have lost* it.
B: Or she *might be doing* some window shopping, you know what she's like.
C: Yes, but I tried phoning her mobile and she didn't answer.
B: She *mustn't have forgotten* it at home. She's always doing that!
A: Or she *may have let* the battery run down again. That's another of her favourite tricks!
C: Well, there's nothing we can do really, except wait. Hold on, is there another exit to the station?
B: Yes, there is.
C: Well, she *may be waiting* for us there!
B: Yes, of course that *must have been* what she's doing! Let's go and have a look!

4 Delete the one incorrect option for each sentence.

1 It *may have / might have / can't have* been the air-conditioning in the first class carriage. It was freezing!
2 It *mustn't have / must have / could have* been the chicken sandwiches I bought on the train.
3 It *can't have been / might have been / wasn't* the water because I brought it with me from home.
4 I think I *must have / couldn't have / might have* caught it from that man who was opposite me, he was coughing all the time.
5 It *must / can't / might be* contagious, I'd better stay at home.
6 I *may / might / must* have to take a few days off work, I'm not sure yet.
7 It *might have / must / could* be the start of an epidemic.
8 It *might be / could be / must have been* on the news – I'd better turn on the TV to see.

5 Look at the photo and complete the sentences.

What happened?
1 He may have _____.
2 He must have _____.
3 He can't have _____.

What's he doing?
4 He might be _____.
5 He can't be _____.
6 He must be _____.

🔘 DICTATION

6 🔘 **22** Write the sentences that you hear.

1 _____ .
2 _____ .
3 _____ .
4 _____ .
5 _____ .
6 _____ .
7 _____ .

8c | Alternative therapies

MODALS (PERMISSION, OBLIGATION & PROHIBITION)

1 Choose the best verb form to complete the text.

There was a time when workers (1) *were allowed to / weren't allowed to* get out of their chairs. They (2) *had to / didn't have to* sit there for up to eight hours a day. They (3) *were allowed to / couldn't* take a ten-minute coffee break, but after that they (4) *had to / didn't need to* ask permission to leave their desks. Now, all that has changed. In modern offices, people (5) *can / must* now leave their work stations without having to ask for permission. Of course, they still (6) *have to / don't need to* get on with their work, but with wifi connections and cordless phones they (7) *are allowed to / don't have to* be at their desks to be at work. In fact, new office regulations should state that workers (8) *mustn't / needn't* sit at their desks for more than forty minutes at a time, and that they (9) *have to / don't have to* get up and stretch their legs, even if it's just for a few minutes.

2 Complete the text with one word in each gap. Contractions (e.g. *isn't*) count as one word.

I work as a pharmacist and as part of the job we (1) _____ to wear a uniform. When I first started, I hated the uniform. We (2) _____ to wear a knee length skirt and tights all year round. We weren't (3) _____ to wear high heels or jewellery, although we (4) _____ allowed to wear earrings, so long as they were small and simple. But things have changed in the ten years I've been working here. We (5) _____ have to wear skirts anymore, we (6) _____ wear trousers if we want, so long as they're smart and clean. But we (7) _____ allowed to wear heavy make-up and any tattoos (8) _____ be covered up.

VOCABULARY FROM THE LESSON

3 Complete the text with the phrases in the box.

> colour scheme   ergonomic keyboard   full spectrum
> growing number   low morale   natural light
> work-related illness

Put some light in your life

Spending long hours every day working in artificial light can quickly result in fatigue and (1) _____. A (2) _____ of companies, as well as schools and colleges, are investing in (3) _____ fluorescent lights which simulate (4) _____.

Change your (5) _____

Therapists advise redecorating your workplace at least once a year. They suggest a combination of calming colours like blue and green to reduce stress.

Look after your back

By far the most common (6) _____ is back pain. Too many of us sit at our desks for too long. Investing in a good chair and using an (7) _____ can help us develop a better posture.

💿 DICTATION

4 💿 **23** Write the sentences that you hear.

1 _____
   _____.

2 _____
   _____.

3 _____
   _____.

4 _____
   _____.

5 _____
   _____.

8D | Back pain

CHANGING THE SUBJECT

1 Complete the dialogues with the words in the box.

for	reminds	talking	think	saying	way

1

A: I was talking to Bob this morning. He says his mother's out of hospital.

B: Oh, that (1) _____ me, did you get a get-well card for Jean?

A: Oh, sorry, I forgot. I'll get one on the way home from work.

B: No, hold on a second. Come to (2) _____ of it, I may have one in the drawer. I bought one for Robert, but I never sent it! Yes, here it is!

2

A: So the boss said we've got to cut back on expenses somehow.

B: (3) _____ of expenses, did you see the new chair she got for her office?

A: Yeah! And as (4) _____ her expenses claim for her last trip abroad, five-star hotels, expensive wines, she even claimed fifty quid for a haircut!

3

A: So we need to get some food in, tidy up the spare room and, oh, by the (5) _____, I found that book you were looking for.

B: Oh great, thanks, where was it?

A: Under the sofa. Anyway, as I was (6) _____, the spare room needs …

"I'll be home early. They all phoned in sick again."

PHRASAL VERBS WITH OBJECTS

2 Replace the verbs in italics with a phrasal verb in the box and make any necessary changes.

call in	drop off	get back to	look after
put off	put up with	sort out	talk through

1 You should *take care of* your back, you know, or you could develop problems later in life.
2 I'll *contact* you later today with times and prices for the massage sessions.
3 I know I should make an appointment to see the dentist, but I keep *thinking of something else I have to do instead.*
4 Can you do me a favour and *leave* this letter at reception on your way out.
5 We're hoping to *ask* a colour therapist to redecorate the work area.
6 I'm sorry, but we just can't *tolerate* that kind of behaviour anymore.
7 They *explained* the treatment to us in great detail.
8 The problem won't just *go away* if you ignore it, you have to do something about it.

3 Find and correct four mistakes in the sentences.

1 They said they'd get me back to with more information about the acupuncture sessions.
2 There's nothing we can do about the noise, so we just have to put it up with.
3 He would never have done that on his own initiative – someone must have put him up to it.
4 I love jogging, but my doctor's said I have to give up it because it's bad for my back.
5 The boss told off him for making personal calls during work hours.
6 By the way, you know that parcel you'd prepared for your mum? Well, I dropped it off at her house last night.

TRANSLATION

4 Translate the dialogue into your language.

Husband: So, how did it go? You know, with the osteopath, how was it?
Wife: Not too bad, actually. I was surprised. It really did seem to make a difference.
Husband: I told you it would.
Wife: I know, I know, I should have started going much sooner. By the way, have you sent off that form for the sports club yet?
Husband: No, not yet, but I will, I'll get on to it this morning.

8 | Reading

1 What stories do you know that begin and end with the following words?

'Once upon a …
… lived happily ever after.'

2 Read the story and put the pictures in the correct order.

☐

☐

☐

☐

3 Read the story again and put the events in the correct order.

☐ The man lied to the police.
☐ *1* The man told his wife what he had seen.
☐ The psychiatrist thought the woman was crazy.
☐ The woman contacted the psychiatrist.
☐ The woman refused to believe her husband.
☐ The woman threatened her husband.

4 Find the phrases 1–7 in the story and choose the best definition, a or b. The line numbers are in brackets.

1 a mythical beast (5)
   a) an animal that has one horn
   b) an animal that only exists in stories

2 a lily (8)
   a) a flower
   b) a piece of sugar

3 he roused his wife (10)
   a) he shouted at her
   b) he woke her up

4 a gloat in her eye (20)
   a) an expression of fear
   b) an expression of happiness

5 a solemn signal (27)
   a) a serious movement with a special meaning
   b) a smile that you cannot control

6 they finally subdued her (29)
   a) they controlled her
   b) they killed her

7 cursing and screaming (34)
   a) shouting in an excited way
   b) using bad language very loudly

5 Who is the crazy person in the story?

💿 READ & LISTEN

6 💿 **24** Listen to Reading 8 *The Unicorn in the Garden* on the CD and read the story again.

The Unicorn in the Garden
by James Thurber (1894–1961)

Once upon a sunny morning, a man who sat in a breakfast nook looked up from his scrambled eggs to see a white unicorn with a golden horn quietly cropping the roses in the garden. The man went up to the bedroom where his wife was still asleep and woke her. 'There's a unicorn in the garden,' he said. 'Eating roses.'

5 She opened one unfriendly eye and looked at him. 'The unicorn is a mythical beast,' she said, and turned her back on him. The man walked slowly downstairs and out into the garden. The unicorn was still there; he was now browsing among the tulips.

'Here, unicorn,' said the man and pulled up a lily and gave it to him. The unicorn ate it gravely. With a high heart, because there was a unicorn in his garden, the man went

10 upstairs and roused his wife again. 'The unicorn,' he said, 'ate a lily.' His wife sat up in bed and looked at him, coldly. 'You are a booby,' she said, 'and I am going to have you put in a booby-hatch.'

The man, who never liked the words 'booby' and 'booby-hatch,' and who liked them even less on a shining morning when there was a unicorn in the garden, thought for a

15 moment. 'We'll see about that,' he said. He walked over to the door. 'He has a golden horn in the middle of his forehead,' he told her. Then he went back to the garden to watch the unicorn; but the unicorn had gone away. The man sat among the roses and went to sleep.

And as soon as the husband had gone out of the house, the wife got up and dressed as

20 fast as she could. She was very excited and there was a gloat in her eye. She telephoned the police and she telephoned the psychiatrist; she told them to hurry to her house and bring a straitjacket. When the police and the psychiatrist arrived, they sat down in chairs and looked at her with great interest.

'My husband,' she said, 'saw a unicorn this morning.' The police looked at the

25 psychiatrist and the psychiatrist looked at the police. 'He told me it ate a lily,' she said. The psychiatrist looked at the police and the police looked at the psychiatrist. 'He told me it had a golden horn in the middle of its forehead,' she said. At a solemn signal from the psychiatrist, the police leaped from their chairs and seized the wife. They had a hard time subduing her, for she put up a terrific struggle, but they finally subdued her. Just as

30 they got her into the straitjacket, the husband came back into the house.

'Did you tell your wife you saw a unicorn?' asked the police. 'Of course not,' said the husband. 'The unicorn is a mythical beast.' 'That's all I wanted to know,' said the psychiatrist. 'Take her away. I'm sorry, sir, but your wife is as crazy as a jay bird.' So they took her away, cursing and screaming, and shut her up in an institution. The husband

35 lived happily ever after.

Moral: Don't count your boobies until they are hatched.

booby /ˈbuːbɪ/ noun [C] *informal old-fashioned* a stupid person
booby-hatch /ˈbuːbɪˈhætʃ/ noun [C] *informal old-fashioned offensive* a hospital for the mentally ill

9A | Celebrity heroes

ADJECTIVE ORDER

1 Insert the adjectives on the right in the correct place in the advertisements 1–8.

1	📷	Italian leather dancing shoes (size 36)	$49.95	stylish
2	📷	4 exceptional-value original 1960s dining chairs. As new.	$195.99	plastic
3	📷	Life-size, full-colour poster of Natalie Portman	$3.99	amazing
4	📷	Unwanted pair of long boxer shorts	$0.99	grey
5	📷	Large black wizard's hat	$4.50	pointed
6	📷	Beautiful miniature Venetian rose	$9.99	glass
7	📷	Enormous (6 X 4m) blue / yellow flag	$4.00	European
8	📷	Brand new Japanese digital camera (8 megapix)	$350.00	super-slim

2 Complete the descriptions of the pictures with the adjectives in the box.

> black   French   grey   huge   long   old
> round   satin   smelly   square   wooden
> woollen

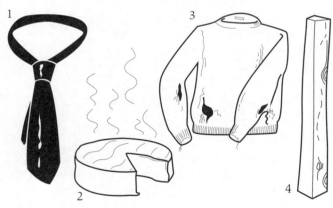

1 a _____, _____, _____ tie

2 a _____, _____, _____ cheese

3 an _____, _____, _____ jumper

4 a _____, _____, _____ stick

VOCABULARY FROM THE LESSON

3 Complete the sentences 1–7 with the phrases a–g.

A

1 Her work is an *all-consuming*
2 I hope you will control your *primitive*
3 It was meant as a *harmless*
4 Most of my friends are *like-minded*
5 She's got a *grotesque*
6 There's no need to be *anxious*
7 We need to protect *impressionable*

B

☐ a about me – I'll be fine.
☐ b children who believe everything they hear.
☐ c instincts when the meal is served.
☐ d joke, so I'm sorry if you were insulted.
☐ e passion – she lives and breathes the law.
☐ f people who see things the way I do.
☐ g poster of a skull and a monster on her wall.

4 Complete the text with prepositions.

Jeremy and I are absolutely obsessed (1) _____ the Eurovision Song Contest and the highlight (2) _____ our year is when all our friends come round and we watch the show together (3) _____ TV. There are usually about thirty (4) _____ us all packed (5) _____ our living room. Jeremy is so devoted (6) _____ the show that he watches all the qualifying competitions on national TV, so it's normal (7) _____ him to be something (8) _____ an expert. Some friends think that our obsession is a cause (9) _____ concern, but I prefer to think (10) _____ it (11) _____ a bit of harmless fun.

💿 DICTATION

5 💿 25 Write the text that you hear.

_____

_____

_____

_____

_____

_____

_____

9B | Local hero

ADJECTIVES WITH PREPOSITIONS

1 Match the words in the box to the definitions 1–8.

> aware   connected   devoted   familiar   intent
> involved   restricted   sympathetic

1 affected by or included in an activity, event or situation _____

2 containing or dealing with one particular thing _____

3 determined to do something _____

4 intended only for people who have been given special permission _____

5 joined to each other or to something else _____

6 knowing about a situation or a fact _____

7 supporting a plan, action, or person _____

8 well known to you or easily recognized by you _____

2 Complete the sentences with an appropriate preposition.

1 Very few people are aware _____ his true identity.

2 His whole life is devoted _____ the fight against crime.

3 Some of the city's top businessmen are involved _____ criminal activities.

4 The fight is not restricted _____ Gotham City.

5 He is fighting for a world that is free _____ evil.

6 He is also intent _____ getting revenge on the murderers of his parents.

7 He has been responsible _____ the capture of many dangerous criminals.

VOCABULARY FROM THE LESSON

3 Complete the sentences with a word in the box.

> check out   citizenship   inconvenience
> psychologist   reveal   sighting   triumphing
> update

1 We all love a good story of good _____ over evil.

2 We apologize for any _____ you may experience during your stay.

3 We can now _____ the identity of the Caped Crusader.

4 We got Canadian _____ three years after applying.

5 We have just been informed that the police have reported another _____ of a UFO.

6 We turn now to our reporter on the scene for the latest _____ on the war.

7 We will, of course, _____ all the details before printing the story.

8 We've decided to see an educational _____ to ask for advice.

TRANSLATION

4 Translate the text into your language.

Like so many superheroes, Peter Parker's parents were killed during his childhood. Peter was brought up by his uncle and aunt and was a shy adolescent, lacking in confidence and popularity. But then, at the age of fifteen, after being bitten by a radioactive spider, Peter developed superhuman strength and the ability to climb up walls. His career as a crime crusader had begun.

9c | Villains

ADVERBS & MODIFYING ADJECTIVES

1 Complete the table with pairs of adjectives in the box.

ancient	~~angry~~	awful	bad	big	boiling
brilliant	cold	crucial	delighted		difficult
enormous	exhausted	fascinated			freezing
~~furious~~	good	happy	hot		important
impossible	interested	old	tired		

gradable	ungradable
angry	_furious_
1 _____	_____
2 _____	_____
3 _____	_____
4 _____	_____
5 _____	_____
6 _____	_____
7 _____	_____
8 _____	_____
9 _____	_____
10 _____	_____
11 _____	_____

2 Choose the best way to complete the dialogues.

1 **A:** That was *completely / pretty* scary, wasn't it?
  B: Scary? It was *absolutely / very* terrifying.
2 **A:** That was *really / totally* tiring, wasn't it?
  B: Absolutely. I'm completely *exhausted / tired*.
3 **A:** That was *a bit / absolutely* difficult, wasn't it?
  B: Actually, I thought it was *quite / totally* easy.
4 **A:** That must have been *a little / absolutely* awful for you!
  B: Not really. It was even *completely / slightly* enjoyable at times.
5 **A:** That looks *absolutely / very* similar to your dress.
  B: Not at all. They're totally *different / similar*.
6 **A:** That was *absolutely / a bit* fascinating, wasn't it?
  B: To be honest, I thought it was *totally / very* impossible to understand.

CRIMES

3 Match the words in the box to the newspaper stories 1–6.

armed robbery	hijacking	kidnapping	mugging
smuggling	vandalism		

1
An elderly lady in Bexhill-on-Sea turned the tables on two young skinheads who pushed her to the ground and attempted to steal her weekly pension. The woman, a former kung-fu instructor, jumped to her feet, hit …

2
Glasgow police are interviewing a man in hospital following a failed raid at a bureau de change. Witnesses say that the man, who was wearing a Zorro mask, shot himself in the foot as he demanded money from the cashier.

3
A man was arrested at Heathrow yesterday when a suitcase full of bottles of whisky fell off his luggage trolley as he was going through customs. A number of the bottles did …

4
Three teenagers have been ordered to do 120 hours of community service after they were caught spraying graffiti on a train at Wembley station. The three had not noticed a security camera …

5
Armed police officers rescued a businessman from a disused factory in Perivale yesterday. The man, who had been held in the factory for four hours by a gang demanding one million pounds for his release, telephoned the police on his mobile phone when his captors went out to buy sandwiches.

6
Passengers and crew on a transatlantic flight on Monday could not control their laughter when a woman stood up, produced a gun from her bag and demanded to be taken to New York. The gun was obviously a plastic toy and the plane was already going to New York.

🌐 DICTATION

4 🌐 **26** Write the text that you hear.

_____

_____

_____

_____

_____

_____

_____

9D | Hate list

COMPOUND NOUNS (JOBS)

1 Match the groups of words 1–8 to the words in the box to make compound nouns.

> agent courier fighter inspector ~~jockey~~
> rep warden worker

1 champion / disc / top ___jockey___
2 insurance / intelligence / travel _____
3 fire / jet / street _____
4 bicycle / drug / motorcycle _____
5 factory / office / rescue _____
6 health / school / tax _____
7 student / telesales / union _____
8 park / prison / traffic _____

2 Complete the sentences with a compound noun from exercise 1.

1 Every time I sit on the grass, a _____ comes along and tells me to get up.
2 When I was at university, there was a union and I was a _____.
3 If I were a _____, I'd only play the songs I like.
4 I'd like to be a _____ so that I could get cheap holidays.
5 It must be strange to be a _____ and spend all day looking for dirt.
6 My uncle was in the Air Force and took me up in a _____.
7 I was at the airport once and saw the customs officers stop a _____.
8 The trapped motorists were so relieved when they heard a _____ calling through the fog.

CONTRAST

3 Put the phrases in the correct order.

- [1] For the last ten months, Zaid has been working as a traffic warden, even though
- [ ] graduating as the best student in his year, Zaid finds that employers in his adopted country do not recognize his qualification even though
- [ ] he has had it translated into English.
- [ ] he is a qualified doctor. He took the job, in spite of
- [ ] he receives financial support from his uncle, he has no choice but to work. Despite
- [ ] the low pay, because he couldn't find anything else. Zaid has a family of four to support, and although

VOCABULARY FROM THE LESSON

4 Complete the definitions with a word in the box.

> arrogant bigoted dashing dazzling
> obnoxious slimy vindictive

1 (*old-fashioned*) a _____ man is attractive and fashionable in an exciting way
2 a _____ light is so bright that it makes you unable to see for a short period of time
3 if something is _____ it is covered with a thick, wet, unpleasant substance
4 someone who is _____ has opinions that most people think are unreasonable, especially about race, politics, or religion, and is not willing to consider other people's opinions
5 someone who is _____ is cruel to anyone who hurts them and will not forgive them
6 someone who is _____ is very rude, offensive, or unpleasant
7 someone who is _____ thinks they are better or more important than other people and behaves in a way that is rude and too confident

TRANSLATION

5 Translate the sentences into your language.

1 What sort of qualifications do you need to become a nightclub bouncer?
2 I think I'll get the job because of my experience as a traffic warden.
3 Despite his lack of communicative skills, he made a fortune as an estate agent.
4 Let's find out what our survey said about English teachers.
5 Although he says he's only doing his job, I think he enjoys handing out parking tickets.
6 When some people find out you're a sales rep, they get really obnoxious.

9 | Reading

1 How much do you know about Batman? Choose the correct answers.

1 Batman lives in
   a) Denver, Colorado.
   b) Metropolis.
   c) Gotham City.

2 Batman's enemies include
   a) the Goodies.
   b) the Joker.
   c) the Teacher.

3 The Batmobile is a special
   a) car.
   b) bicycle.
   c) mobile phone.

4 Batman's badge is
   a) yellow and black.
   b) pink and black.
   c) white and black.

5 Batman has a
   a) dog.
   b) servant.
   c) younger brother called Alfred.

6 Batman changes into his costume in
   a) telephone boxes.
   b) the men's room.
   c) the Batcave.

7 Batman and Robin are sometimes called
   a) the Batgirls.
   b) the Dynamic Duo.
   c) the Vampires.

2 Read the article and choose the best title, 1, 2 or 3.

1 The history of Batman and Robin
2 Buying Batman: a collector's guide
3 POW! Batman's universal appeal

3 The sentences a–e were cut from the end of each paragraph of the article. Match the sentences to the paragraphs 1–5.

☐ a And the batcave is a cave of wonders, full of strange machines with flashing lights and all kinds of tempting levers and buttons to press and pull.

☐ b And so, night after night, he works in the shadows bringing criminals to justice and trying desperately to overcome the trauma that marked his childhood.

☐ c But what is the secret of his appeal?

☐ d And so long as one kid in the neighbourhood has got the newest bat present, everyone else is going to want one too.

☐ e These are the same people who spend millions of pounds collecting Batman memorabilia: first issue comic books, limited issue toys and all sorts of gadgets.

4 Read the article again. In which paragraph(s) 1–5 can you find the information a–h?

☐ a Selling Batman toys and costumes to children is very profitable.
☐ b A lot of superheroes disappeared after the 1950s.
☐ c The original Batman only came out at night.
☐ d A lot of Batman merchandise is targeted at an adult audience.
☐ e Not all Batman merchandise is original.
☐ f Very young children like Batman too.
☐ g Batman appeals to both adults and children.
☐ h Batman shows human weaknesses.

5 Match the verb phrases in bold in the text to one of the words or phrases 1–6.

1 full of   4 go to in large numbers
2 possess   5 appeared in public
3 has a lot of   6 find

6 Why does Batman appeal more to boys than to girls?

🔘 READ & LISTEN

7 🔘 **27** Listen to Reading 9 *Batman* on the CD and read the article again.

1 Batman first appeared in May, 1939. He was one of a host of superheroes who were fighting to bring peace to the streets of American cities. But, unlike most of the hundreds of costumed crime fighters that **took to the streets** between the 1930s and 1950s, Batman survived well into the 21st century and he is now possibly the world's most popular superhero. He is certainly number one in the field of superhero merchandising. There are more than 1,000 bat-items licensed for sale in the US, and probably just as many cheap imitations. You can buy all sorts of things, from dolls and costumes to clocks, perfume and inflatable beds.

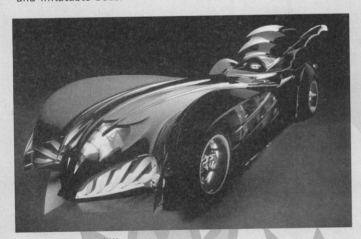

Batman memorabilia

2 Like all good heroes, Batman is not perfect. He is eaten up by revenge: revenge for the deaths of his own parents and for those of the 'boy wonder', Robin. He and Robin manage to capture Antonio Zucco, the gangland boss who was responsible for the deaths of Robin's parents, but Batman will never be able to **track down** the criminal who killed his own parents in cold blood.

3 He hides his obsession behind a mask and **is plagued by** doubts. Who is he? Which is his true identity? Is he the philanthropist millionaire Bruce Wayne or the masked vigilante working in the shadows? Bruce Wayne spends his days putting his money to work to help the poor and needy, but at night he takes the law into his own hands and sometimes comes very close to crossing the thin line between crime and crime fighting. This is the Batman that appeals to the adult readers of the DC comics, and the adult audiences that **flock to** the cinemas to see the Batman films.

4 But there's another Batman too. One who works by day, whose punches and kicks are accompanied by cartoon 'POW's and 'KERPLUNK's. The Batman of the cult 1960s TV series, shown all over the world and appealing to an adult sense of humour, as well as to the superhero fantasies of much younger viewers. To these younger kids he's just one of them, with an envious choice of great toys to play with: batmobiles, batbikes, bathelicopters, batboats, batjets, you name it – he's got one.

5 What three-year-old wouldn't want to **get their hands on** all those goodies? The Batman merchandising machine has known how to make the most of this very lucrative market and Batman's appeal has grown and grown and grown. Bat toys and costumes are available for kids as young as three years old and parks and playgrounds across the world are **peopled with** miniature batpeople.

'I like Batman 'cos he fights crime and his ears stick up' (Sam, aged 3)

10A | Good deeds

REFLEXIVE VERBS

1 Replace the words in italics with a phrase in the box.

> adapt yourself to   expressed yourself
> content yourself   distinguish yourself
> ask yourself   you should consider yourself

1 *I think you were* lucky, it could have been much worse.
2 *Think about* what would be better, to lose or not to have tried at all.
3 You need to learn to *cope with* new situations or you'll end up having a nervous breakdown!
4 Congratulations, I think you *put your ideas into words* really well.
5 If you can't change a situation then the best thing is to learn to *be happy* with it.
6 If you want to *be successful* as an artist, you're going to have to work much harder.

2 Add the reflexive pronoun *themselves* to the text where necessary (7 times).

It is natural that parents endanger in order to protect their young, both in the human and animal world. But this decision to sacrifice for their children is not always the best choice. How will the children survive without their parents if they are too young to look after? Parents need to remind that they need to look after their own safety first, so that they are then in a better position to look after that of their children. This is also true in day-to-day life. Parents who dedicate not only to their children, but also to their other interests and passions, make better parents. They should not consider to be the slaves of their children, but rather pride on being happy, satisfied individuals who share their love of life with their family.

VOCABULARY FROM THE LESSON

3 Complete the questions with a preposition in the box.

> against   for   from (x2)   to (x2)

1 What exactly is it that **sets us apart** _____ the beasts?

2 Do you **attach great importance** _____ material goods?

3 Are you willing to **sacrifice yourself** _____ a good cause?

4 Will they ever be able **to provide an answer** _____ the question?

5 Would you ever consider **giving evidence** _____ your best friend?

6 Do you think you would **benefit** _____ a holiday?

4 Complete the sentences with the expressions in bold in exercise 3.

1 I think this room would really _____ a complete makeover.

2 My grandparents _____ their independence and never like asking for help.

3 The ability to control our tempers is another thing that _____ primitive man.

4 The jury listened attentively as she _____ her ex-husband.

5 There's no need for you to _____ for your job. The company would never do the same for you.

6 We believe we can _____ your problem.

TRANSLATION

5 Translate the proverbs into your language.

1 Actions speak louder than words.
2 Saying is one thing, and doing, another.
3 A good deed is never lost.
4 Easier said than done.
5 One good deed deserves another.
6 The evil that men do lives after them.
7 It is not how long, but how well we live our lives.

10B | Giving

REPORTING

1 Rearrange the words in brackets to complete the sentences.

1 She asked him (*wanted the jacket to keep if he him for her*)

_____ .

2 He said (*he'd later back for it afternoon come that*) _____

_____ .

3 They told us (*charity giving they to it were*)

_____ .

4 We asked them (*they'd coming be back day next the whether*) _____ .

5 He told them (*couple days of he away for a going might be*) _____ .

6 She asked him (*thought when getting back he he'd be*) _____ .

7 He said (*finished with want it it he'd and didn't anymore*) _____ .

2 Change the sentences in exercise 1 into direct speech.

3 Find and correct six mistakes in the text.

I asked him where was his new jacket and why wasn't he wearing it. He said it had been stolen from his office. I asked him why hadn't he told me and he said he doesn't want to upset me. When I told him I had known the truth, he said was he really sorry, he hadn't liked the jacket from the start, but he didn't know how to tell me.

4 Complete the report of the dialogue.

1 'We found your jacket.'
2 'Did you know about the money in the pocket?'
3 'I was going to use it to pay a builder.'
4 'Have you got the money with you?'
5 'How much money did you leave in the pocket?'
6 'There should be two thousand pounds in twenty-pound notes.'
7 'Why did you throw the jacket away?'
8 'I didn't throw it away, it was my ex-girlfriend who threw it away. '

She told him that (1) _____ and she asked him (2) _____. He said (3) _____ and he asked (4) _____. She asked him (5) _____. He told her (6) _____ and she asked him (7) _____. He explained that (8) _____.

"I'm not asking you, Mister, I'm telling you!"

COLLOCATIONS WITH *GIVE*

5 Complete the sentences with a word in the box.

> consideration   lecture   permission   priority
> piece of my mind   problems   speech   warning

1 I'll give it top _____ and do it right away.

2 We won't decide now but we'll give your idea some _____.

3 This car's been giving us _____ for ages now, I think we should get rid of it.

4 I'm feeling really nervous – I've got to give a _____ at the dinner.

5 He refused to give _____ to film on his premises.

6 His father gave him a _____ about the dangers of alcohol abuse.

7 People get into trouble there every year, even though they're given plenty of _____ about the dangerous currents.

8 He really shouldn't have done that. I'm going to give him a _____!

🔘 DICTATION

6 🔘 **28** Write the text that you hear.

_____

_____

_____

_____

_____

10c | Aid worker

JOB RESPONSIBILITIES

1 Complete the verbs with vowels to form verbs often used in job descriptions.

1 p r _ m _ t _
2 l _ _ _ s _
3 _ v _ r s _ _
4 p _ r t _ c _ p _ t _
5 c _ _ r d _ n _ t _
6 t r _ c k
7 s _ _ k   _ _ t
8 f _ c _ l _ t _ t _

2 Replace the words in italics with a verb from exercise 1.

1 I was asked to *take part* in an international aid conference.
2 I had to *act as a messenger* between the headquarters and the grass-roots workers.
3 I often need to *check and sometimes correct* the writing of promotional materials.
4 One of my responsibilities is to *look for* new volunteers.
5 We attempt to *help local groups to overcome problems with* decision making.
6 A key part of my job is to *attract people's attention to* local events and projects.
7 Someone needs to *organize* the work of the various departments and volunteers so that they work efficiently together.
8 We *follow* the progress of all new projects very closely in the first year.

REPORTING VERBS & PATTERNS

3 Report the direct speech with the verbs given.

1 'We don't want to have anything to do with the project.'
   They refused _____.
2 'We're thinking of visiting your site in the North.'
   He mentioned _____.
3 'I really don't know much about recent developments.'
   She admitted _____.
4 'You really must come and see our new offices.'
   They invited us _____.
5 'I'll pass the information on as quickly as possible.'
   He promised _____.
6 'The company has no connection whatsoever with the local authorities.'
   They denied _____.
7 'I really think you should try again.'
   She encouraged me _____.
8 'Don't travel through the mountains after dark.'
   They warned us _____.

4 Find and correct four mistakes in the text.

After lengthy talks with our delegates, the local education authority has agreed opening four new schools in the area. We have managed to persuade them putting forward 50% of the funding and we have suggested to spend this money on the school buildings. In return the education authorities have asked us supplying the teaching staff and materials.

DICTATION

5 🔘 **29** Write the text that you hear.

_____
_____
_____
_____
_____
_____
_____
_____

10D | A good job

JOB INTERVIEWS

1 Complete the texts with one word in each gap.

1 I know I have a tendency (a) _____ take on too much work and I need to learn to delegate more.

2 I've been working (b) _____ the voluntary sector (c) _____ the last five years. To start (d) _____, I worked (e) _____ a volunteer at a charity shop and then gradually worked up to being regional manager.

3 I think this job would give me the chance (f) _____ develop my interpersonal skills.

4 I'm usually good (g) _____ motivating staff and I take pride (h) _____ my ability (i) _____ initiate and manage change and innovation.

5 Mainly my experience in similar projects. I've worked (j) _____ various projects where I've been successful in implementing structural changes.

2 Match the questions a–e to the responses 1–5 in exercise 1.

☐ a Can you tell us something about your work experience to date?
☐ b Why are you interested in the post?
☐ c What do you think you can bring to this job?
☐ d What do you see as your strengths?
☐ e And what about your weaknesses?

VOCABULARY FROM THE LESSON

3 Complete the dialogues with an appropriate form of the verbs in the box.

attend   develop   give   meet   set   write

1 **A:** How's the new job going?
   B: Fine, a bit stressful, there are so many deadlines to (1) _____. And they're all impossible!

2 **A:** I'm going to New York at the weekend.
   B: Wow! Really?
   A: Yeah, I'm (2) _____ a conference.
   B: Are you (3) _____ a talk?
   A: No! Thank goodness!

3 **A:** I had a chat with my boss today.
   B: And?
   A: She says I've got to learn to be more organized, (4) _____ priorities, that kind of thing.

4 **A:** How come you're so late?
   B: We had to (5) _____ a last-minute press release.
   A: Oh yeah, what had happened?

5 **A:** So are you really going to take the job, then?
   B: Yeah, I know it isn't a great job, but at least I'll get a chance to (6) _____ my computer skills.

TRANSLATION

4 Translate the text into your language.

Job interview etiquette

Remember that you should always:

- Arrive about 10 minutes early. If you are running late, phone the company.
- Turn your mobile phone off before you go into the interview room.
- Greet the interviewer by title (Ms, Mr, Dr) and last name. If you're not sure of the pronunciation, ask the receptionist before going into the interview.
- Wait for the interviewer to offer you a seat before you sit down.
- Send a thank-you email or letter to your interviewer within 24 hours of the interview.

www.CartoonStock.com

"Number four wasn't too bad – at least he removed his personal CD earphones for most of the interview."

10 | Reading

1 Look at the webpage on page 63. How many times do you think people visit this website every year?

1 Over 100, 000 times.
2 Over 250,000 times.
3 Over 500,000 times.

2 Look at the extracts A–E from the website. Match them to the hyperlinks in the left-hand column (*What you can do*) on the webpage.

3 Read the extracts A–E again. Which of the following ways of supporting Oxfam are mentioned?

a buying stuff from the website
b cycling from London to Brighton
c collecting stamps
d giving blood
e giving your old computer to Oxfam
f making a regular donation
g persuading your company to sponsor Oxfam
h taking part in a special event
i using an Oxfam credit card
j volunteering to work in a shop

Oxfam

4 Explain the phrases 1–6 in your own words. The line numbers are in brackets.

1 retail outlet (4)
2 a rare first edition (9)
3 work their own way out of (24)
4 the duration of the challenge (29)
5 you've moved on (35)
6 each working donated handset (45)

🔊 📖 READ & LISTEN

5 📀 📖 **30** Listen to Reading 10 *Oxfam* on the CD and read the website extracts again.

C

25

What is Trailwalker?

Trailwalker UK is a 100km trek across the South Downs of England, starting in Petersfield and ending in Brighton. You and three friends have 30 hours to complete the trek and you must stay together as a team for the duration of the challenge.

30

Trailwalker will give you a huge sense of achievement, it's a great way to get fit, and an opportunity to help some of the world's poorest people.

A

If you have a spare afternoon or two or even more, you could join the dedicated team of professionals and supporters at your local Oxfam shop. There is arguably more skill and scope in working in an Oxfam shop than any other retail outlet in the high street.

5

Whilst Oxfam shops do sell a range of new products – cards, gifts, food etc – the majority of the stock is donated to the shops by Oxfam's supporters. So you never know what is going out on the shop floor, how much it will be or whether you are going to discover a valuable antique or a rare first edition.

D

Oxfam can turn unwanted mobile phones and their accessories into money to support work with people all over the world.

35

You know how it is – you've moved on. You're now with the latest model, and your old mobile phone, the one you used to love and take everywhere with you, is left at home, unwanted and abandoned. On the shelf.

40

But it doesn't have to be like this ... your old mobile can have a new life, full of meaning and purpose. On average, each

45

working donated handset is worth £5 to Oxfam – but some are worth much more.

B

10

£2 each week
can buy 133 school dinners each month. Providing hungry children with nourishing meals to help them to concentrate.

£8 each month

15

can buy a mosquito net. Helping to save lives by preventing the spread of diseases like malaria and yellow fever.

£20 each month
can feed a child orphaned by AIDS in Malawi for three and a half months.

20

£50 each month
can pay a trainee teacher's salary in Kenya for five weeks. Education gives people the skills they need to work their own way out of poverty.

E

Since 1994, Oxfam supporters have raised over £2 million for Oxfam's work overseas, simply by using their Oxfam Visa credit cards.

50

... help Oxfam raise the next £1 million

For every new account opened, the Co-operative Bank will donate £15 to Oxfam.

Oxfam will receive a further £2.50 if the card is used within six months, and 25p for every £100 spent using the card or transferred on to it.

55

Think what a difference you could make – just £15 could buy a desk for a school in Zambia, or a goat for a family in Rwanda.

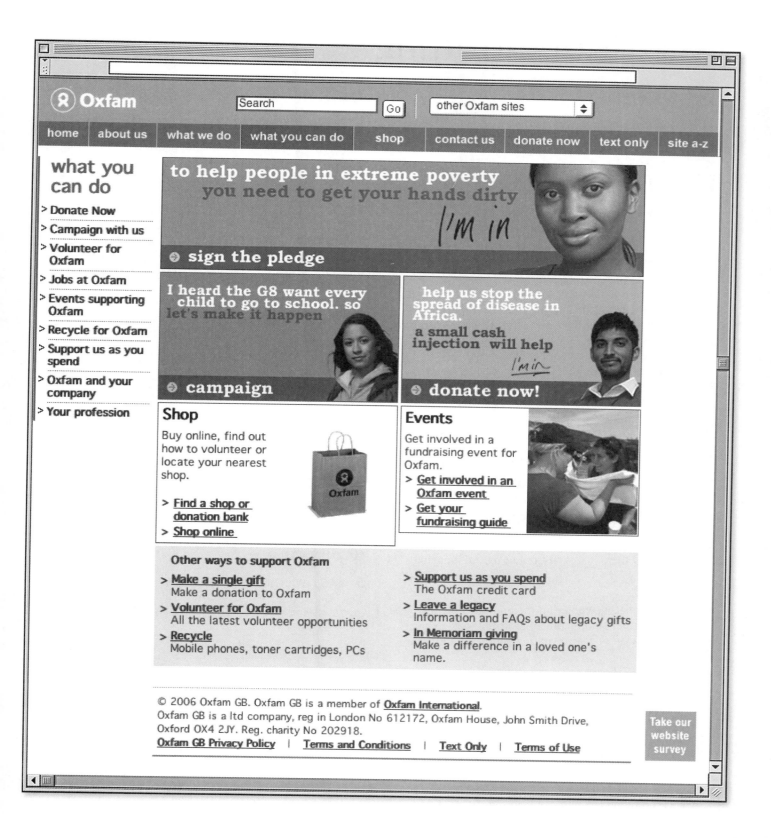

Oxfam

Search [   ] Go | other Oxfam sites ▼

home | about us | what we do | what you can do | shop | contact us | donate now | text only | site a-z

what you can do

> Donate Now
> Campaign with us
> Volunteer for Oxfam
> Jobs at Oxfam
> Events supporting Oxfam
> Recycle for Oxfam
> Support us as you spend
> Oxfam and your company
> Your profession

to help people in extreme poverty you need to get your hands dirty
I'm in

⊕ **sign the pledge**

I heard the G8 want every child to go to school. so let's make it happen

⊕ **campaign**

help us stop the spread of disease in Africa.
a small cash injection will help
I'm in

⊕ **donate now!**

Shop

Buy online, find out how to volunteer or locate your nearest shop.

> **Find a shop or donation bank**
> **Shop online**

Events

Get involved in a fundraising event for Oxfam.

> **Get involved in an Oxfam event**
> **Get your fundraising guide**

Other ways to support Oxfam

> **Make a single gift**
Make a donation to Oxfam

> **Volunteer for Oxfam**
All the latest volunteer opportunities

> **Recycle**
Mobile phones, toner cartridges, PCs

> **Support us as you spend**
The Oxfam credit card

> **Leave a legacy**
Information and FAQs about legacy gifts

> **In Memoriam giving**
Make a difference in a loved one's name.

Take our website survey

11A | Globe-trotting

GEOGRAPHICAL FEATURES

1 Match the words in the box to their dictionary definitions 1–8.

> bay   canal   cape   desert   falls   ocean
> peninsula   strait

1   a long piece of land mostly surrounded by water _____
2   one of the large areas of salt water that cover most of the Earth _____
3   an artificial river _____
4   a large area of land that continues further out into the sea than the land it is part of _____
5   a place where water flows over the edge of a cliff, rock, or other steep place _____
6   an area of the coast where the land curves inwards _____
7   a large area of land with few plants and little water and where the weather is always dry _____
8   a narrow area of water that joins two larger areas of water _____

2 Match the descriptions to six of the words in the box in exercise 1.

1   It took us eight days to cross it from East to West. The heat during the day was almost unbearable.

2   We heard it before we saw it, an incredible thundering noise – and there it was in front of us. An amazing sight.

3   There's a great viewpoint on the Spanish side, just west of Gibraltar. The mountains of Morocco look so close across the strip of sea separating Africa from Europe.

4   We climbed over the top of the hill and there it was in front of us. Almost a perfect semicircle with a tiny whitewashed fishing village right at the water's edge.

5   The boats lined up, ready to go through the first of five locks which would take us up 40m to the next stretch of water.

6   We sat on the beach and watched the sun go down as the waves lapped gently against the rocks.

THE & GEOGRAPHICAL NAMES

3 Find and delete five unnecessary uses of *the* in the text.

The Straits of Magellan are named after the Portuguese explorer who first sailed through this narrow passage connecting the Atlantic and the Pacific. The Straits lead from the border between the Chile and the Argentina in the East, past the town of the Punta Arenas to the islands of the Queen Adelaide Archipelago in the West. It was the only safe route between the two oceans until 1914 when the Panama Canal was opened, enabling ships to sail right through the Central America. It was a popular route with prospectors trying to reach the coast of the California in the 1849 Gold Rush.

4 Add *the* in the gaps where necessary.

The cruise was incredible. Out of this world. We set off from the town of (1) _____ Ushaia, the world's southernmost city in the foothills of (2) _____ Andes. Then we sailed through (3) _____ Drake Passage out into (4) _____ Antarctic Ocean, turning our backs on (5) _____ South America. We were heading for (6) _____ South Shetland Islands at the tip of (7) _____ Antarctic Peninsula, an amazing strip of ice with the most spectacular glaciers practically falling into the sea. And there were lots of penguins too!

⊙ DICTATION

5 ⊙ **31** Write the sentences that you hear.

1   _____ .
2   _____ .
3   _____
    _____ .
4   _____
    _____ .
5   _____ .

11B | South is up

BINOMIALS

1 There are mistakes in four of the phrases in *italics* in the sentences. Find and correct them.

1 The golden rule of public speaking is always to keep it *sweet and short*. _____

2 He worked *long and hard* to get to where he is today. _____

3 His study is an amazing place, it's full of *pieces and bits* from all over the world. _____

4 It's always better to put things down in *white and black* so you've got a record of the decisions taken. _____

5 He was *born and bred* in Scotland, but spends most of his time on the French Riviera. _____

6 Try not to get too angry and remember it's always better to *forget and forgive*. _____

2 Complete the texts with the words in the box.

blood	choose	flesh	fro	here	now	pick
tested	to	tried				

```
1. Happy Homes  Consumer Guide _____ and
   _____
   We put 20 vacuum cleaners through their steps to see which
   came out on top …

2. Gardener's World, New Catalogue
   _____ and _____ from a wide range of plants,
   trees and shrubs.

3. _____ and _____ between London and New
   York, the hazards of frequent flying
   Jane Brown shares her experiences of the two cities in …

4. Movie review: My _____ and _____
   Winner of the Audience and Director's Awards at the
   Sundance Festival, the film follows one remarkable family's
   most …

5. Techniques for managing stress, stress tips, stress guides,
   stress …
   Immediate solutions _____ and _____!
```

VAGUE LANGUAGE

3 Shorten the text by deleting all the vague language.

It's kind of difficult to say exactly what it is to be Australian. People talk about national identity and stuff like that, but it's really much more personal. It's stuff like the things you do every day, your family, your friends and so on and the things you do together. The way we live our lives sort of defines who we are, and I suppose there is a lifestyle which could be called more or less typically Australian. It's a simple lifestyle, an outdoor lifestyle. It doesn't mean we're all sports mad, surfing or kayaking or something all day long, but it does mean that we tend to spend a lot of time outside, you know, in our gardens, on the beach, taking it easy.

4 Add the words in the box to the text.

know	like	of (x 2)	on	or (x 2)	so

I've loved maps since I was a kid. I suppose they kind remind me of my dad. He had a huge one in his study. It covered the whole wall. It must have been like 5 metres long something. We used to spend hours just, you, looking at the map and planning imaginary journeys and stuff that. We used to stick flags in it to show where we'd been on holiday and so. And since I left home I've always, more less, had a map in my room. And my bookshelves are packed with them, road maps, street maps, atlases, globes and on. Some people say I'm obsessed and I guess they're sort right.

TRANSLATION

5 Translate the text into your language.

My favourite place is a small fishing village in Cornwall. I first went there when I was ten years old or so. We used to go there on family holidays, more or less every summer. It was a great place for kids with rockpools and hidden beaches and all that kind of stuff. But I still love it as an adult. Now I'm more into the surf and the seafood restaurants and that kind of thing, you know, adult stuff.

11c | Positive psychology

ARTICLES

1 Choose the correct options to complete the text.

What makes you happy?
Our readers answered (1) *a* / *the* question.

Jean: Spending some time on my own, listening to (2) *the* / *Ø* music, reading (3) *a* / *the* magazine, or simply sitting on (4) *the* / *Ø* sofa!

Roy: When (5) *a* / *the* kids come to visit, seeing them play in (6) *a* / *the* garden, watching them as they run and shout … and (7) *the* / *Ø* wonderful silence in (8) *an* / *the* house when they've gone home!

Nick: Going for (9) *a* / *the* jog in (10) *the* / *Ø* park after (11) *a* / *Ø* work, drinking (12) *a* / *the* cup of (13) *the* / *Ø* tea as I read my newspaper.

Kay: (14) *The* / *Ø* travelling, visiting (15) *the* / *Ø* new places, meeting (16) *the* / *Ø* new people and looking at (17) *a* / *the* photos when (18) *a* / *the* holiday's over!

2 Find and delete seven unnecessary articles in the text.

What is happiness? The secret's in the 'flow'

Researchers believe that happiness, or 'a life satisfaction' occurs most frequently when people lose themselves in the daily activities. The term used to describe this is 'flow'. A people in flow may be doing something very simple, sewing a button on a shirt or cooking a meal. They may be involved in a work, playing a musical instrument, taking part in the sport or losing themselves in a good book. The result is always the same.

The important thing is to identify the activities in your a day-to-day life that absorb you most and to build your life around these things. That, it seems, is the secret of the true happiness.

VOCABULARY FROM THE LESSON

3 Rewrite the sentences with the word or phrase in brackets.

1 Very often other people's opinions of us are much more important than our bank balance. (*perceptions*)
2 There is no simple, straightforward relationship between happiness and money. (*correlation*)
3 It is very important to take a number of different factors into account. (*crucial*)
4 It is also important to remember that we are looking at overall happiness and not single extremely happy moments. (*euphoric*)
5 But having measured happiness levels, we still need to deal with the basic problem of finding ways of making people happier. (*tackle*)
6 The wealthiest people in society are not necessarily the happiest. (*affluent*)

TRANSLATION

4 Translate the text into your language.

Today, it is claimed, is the happiest day of the year. Researchers claim that a combination of good weather, the proximity of the summer holidays, long light evenings and plenty of outdoor activities are responsible for the nation's happiest day this year. Earlier this year they claimed that January 23rd was the most depressing day of the year, with the Christmas holidays almost forgotten, the long-awaited January payslip still a week away and dark, cold nights keeping everybody indoors.

11D | Perfect locations

DESCRIBING LANDSCAPE

1 Complete the texts with the words in the box.

> cliffs   estuary   gorge   hills   peaks   valleys

The closing scene shows our heroine running barefoot across a wide sandy (1) _____.

The gentle, rolling (2) _____ and fertile, wooded (3) _____ are a perfect backdrop for this adaptation of the famous Shakespeare comedy.

The main action takes place inside a deep, narrow (4) _____, hidden from the outside world, where the time travellers come face-to-face with a range of prehistoric animals.

The jagged, snowy (5) _____ and the tall, steep (6) _____ of the Rocky Mountains are as much the stars of this action movie as the actors themselves.

SO & SUCH

2 Choose the correct words to complete the text.

Have you ever wondered how sci-fi movie makers create (1) *so / such* incredible new worlds? Read on and find out. It's not (2) *so / such* difficult, all you have to do is look around you – and be prepared to travel!

Star Wars is set in 'a galaxy far, far way', but you too can visit the far away planets that have become (3) *so / such* famous on the big screen. Luke Skywalker's home, Tatouine, which looks (4) *so / such* strange, (5) *so / such* much like it's on another planet, is based on a village in Tunisia.

Matmata is (6) *so / such* a beautiful spot that it was already popular with tourists, and Luke's home in the film is actually a hotel.

3 Rewrite the sentences with the words in brackets.

1 It's been a long time since I've seen a really good film. (*such*)
2 The scenery was incredibly beautiful, it was almost a distraction from the film. (*so ... that*)
3 The story is very simple. (*such*)
4 But the acting is extremely good and it really brings the story alive (*so ... that*)
5 The closing scene was one of the saddest I've ever seen, it made me cry. (*so*)
6 It's a truly excellent movie and I highly recommend it. (*such*)

🔘 DICTATION

4 🔘 **32** Write the conversation that you hear.

A: _____

B: _____

A: _____

B: _____

A: _____

B: _____

11 | Reading

1 Read the article and put the paragraphs A–D in the correct order in the table.

PARA	1	2	3	4	5	6
	■					■

2 Read the article again. In which paragraphs 1–6 can you find the information a–h?

a It is possible for everyone to be happier.

b People are happier when they feel that they belong to a group.

c People's happiness was evaluated a number of times during the experiment.

d Slough is often considered to be an unattractive place to live.

e Some activities took place in the countryside near Slough.

f The aim of the experiment was to find out if happiness could be increased in the town.

g The experts had not expected the experiment to work so well.

h The volunteers worked with artists and musicians for a performance at the end of the project.

3 Find the words and expressions 1–7 in the article and choose the correct definition, a or b. The line numbers are in brackets.

1 dull (9)
   a) boring
   b) interesting

2 soaring (17)
   a) decreasing very quickly
   b) increasing very quickly

3 resounding (20)
   a) complete
   b) incomplete

4 turn around (29)
   a) start being successful
   b) stop being successful

5 literally (34)
   a) an exaggeration of the number
   b) the exact number

6 commune (52)
   a) communicate with words
   b) communicate without words

7 over the course of (60)
   a) after
   b) during

4 Look at the information on a web search engine. On which of the websites could you find more information about the experiment described in the article?

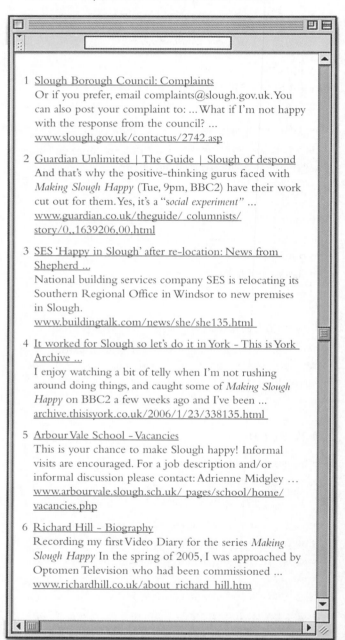

1 <u>Slough Borough Council: Complaints</u>
Or if you prefer, email complaints@slough.gov.uk. You can also post your complaint to: ... What if I'm not happy with the response from the council? ...
<u>www.slough.gov.uk/contactus/2742.asp</u>

2 <u>Guardian Unlimited | The Guide | Slough of despond</u>
And that's why the positive-thinking gurus faced with *Making Slough Happy* (Tue, 9pm, BBC2) have their work cut out for them. Yes, it's a "*social experiment*" ...
<u>www.guardian.co.uk/theguide/ columnists/ story/0,,1639206,00.html</u>

3 <u>SES 'Happy in Slough' after re-location: News from Shepherd ...</u>
National building services company SES is relocating its Southern Regional Office in Windsor to new premises in Slough.
<u>www.buildingtalk.com/news/she/she135.html</u>

4 <u>It worked for Slough so let's do it in York - This is York Archive ...</u>
I enjoy watching a bit of telly when I'm not rushing around doing things, and caught some of *Making Slough Happy* on BBC2 a few weeks ago and I've been ...
<u>archive.thisisyork.co.uk/2006/1/23/338135.html</u>

5 <u>Arbour Vale School - Vacancies</u>
This is your chance to make Slough happy! Informal visits are encouraged. For a job description and/or informal discussion please contact: Adrienne Midgley ...
<u>www.arbourvale.slough.sch.uk/ pages/school/home/ vacancies.php</u>

6 <u>Richard Hill - Biography</u>
Recording my first Video Diary for the series *Making Slough Happy* In the spring of 2005, I was approached by Optomen Television who had been commissioned ...
<u>www.richardhill.co.uk/about richard hill.htm</u>

5 Do you think a similar experiment would work in your town? Why or why not?

READ & LISTEN

6 **33** Listen to Reading 11 *Making Slough Happy* on the CD and read the article again.

Making *Slough* Happy

1

Slough is a modern, commuter town, 20 miles west of London, and although it is really no different from any other satellite town on the commuter routes to London, it has gained an unfortunate reputation for being both ugly and boring. The name, which means a muddy field, certainly doesn't help, nor does its portrayal in the TV comedy show, *The Office*, where it was shown as being dull and depressing. And it was no surprise when a questionnaire showed that the levels of happiness in Slough were well below the national average.

A ☐

As the experiment drew to a close the final questionnaires were distributed. The experts were surprised and delighted by the results. The overall happiness ratings of the group had increased by more than 30%, soaring way above the national UK average. If Slough were a country, it would be the happiest country in the world! The experiment had been a resounding success.

B ☐

So last summer, a team of happiness experts arrived in town. Their aim was to conduct a social experiment, to see if they could make the people of Slough happier. The science of happiness claims that anyone, no matter how happy they are already, can become happier by adopting a few small lifestyle changes and developing a more positive attitude. The team had three months to turn the town around and their work was filmed for a BBC documentary.

C ☐

Towards the end of the three months, they all came together to stage a Grand Finale. A group of the volunteers, helped and supported by artist Helen Marshall, took literally thousands of photos of day-to-day life in Slough and put them together to create an enormous collage of a happy, smiling face. Another group trained to sing an anthem that had been written specifically for the occasion. And a number of local youth groups (a Caribbean drumming band and an Indian dance group, amongst others) joined them on the day of the Grand Finale to stage a free karaoke concert in the middle of Slough town centre.

D ☐

They chose 50 volunteers to help them with their experiment. The volunteers took part in a series of activities and events and their levels of happiness were measured at regular intervals. The activities included camping overnight in nearby woods, dancing in the aisles of a local supermarket and learning to sing. The volunteers experienced the power of saying thank you, of smiling at strangers and of taking time out to commune with nature. They experimented with laughter therapy and learnt to enjoy housework.

6

But what exactly had the experiment shown? That if we sing as we work and smile at strangers, the world will be a happier place? Possibly. But the real success of the experiment had much more to do with the sense of community and purpose that developed over the course of the project than any of the individual activities. The experiment was a success because the people who took part in it felt they were doing something important. They felt valued and useful. This is the key to real happiness.

12A | Loot

PASSIVES REVIEW

1 Choose the best verb form to complete the text.

Most valuable natural pearl necklace

A single-strand pearl necklace which (1) *reputedly wore / was reputedly worn* by French queen Marie-Antoinette (2) *auctioned / was auctioned* for €910,313 ($1,476,345) at Christie's, Geneva, Switzerland, on 16 November 1999. It (3) *was / was been* the highest price that (4) *had ever paid / had ever been paid* for a natural pearl necklace. It (5) *consists / is consisted* of 41 large pearls and it (6) *held / is held* together by a diamond cluster clasp. The necklace (7) *once owned / was once owned* by Woolworth heiress Barbara Hutton (USA). It (8) *bought / was bought* by an anonymous European buyer.

2 Complete the text with the past simple or present perfect passive forms of the verbs in brackets.

---

8 things you didn't know about *Treasure Island*

1 More than 50 movie versions _____ (*make*) of the book.

2 It _____ (*first publish*) in instalments in a children's magazine.

3 It _____ (*adapt*) for both TV and the stage.

4 The first three chapters _____ (*write*) in three days.

5 They _____ (*then read*) aloud to the author's family, who made suggestions for improvements.

6 It _____ (*translate*) into over 25 languages.

7 The author, Stevenson, _____ (*pay*) 100 pounds for the book.

8 It seems that treasure maps with an X showing the treasure _____ (*never use*) by pirates.

VOCABULARY FROM THE LESSON

3 Complete the text with the verbs and phrases in the box.

> carry out   head for   make off with   raid
> threaten   track down

Modern day pirates

Pirates still exist today, and although they don't
(1) _____ coastal towns anymore or
(2) _____ buried treasure, they continue to attack passing ships and (3) _____ as much loot as possible. Modern-day pirates use small boats which are often disguised as fishing boats, and they often
(4) _____ their raids against large cargo ships, which have to slow down as they
(5) _____ narrow channels such as the Suez Canal or the Straits of Malacca. They board the ships,
(6) _____ the crew with violence and grab the contents of the ship's safe. Sometimes the pirates take over the ship and sail it to a nearby port, where it is repainted and given a new identity.

DICTATION

4 🔘 **34** Write the sentences that you hear.

1 _____
  _____
2 _____
  _____
3 _____
  _____
4 _____
  _____

12B | Bounty hunter

IDIOMS (MONEY)

1 Find and insert six missing words in the story.

From rags to riches

Seven years ago Jayne Bingley didn't have a penny her name. She was living from hand mouth and struggling to pay the rent at the end of the month. Now she lives in the lap luxury and has money burn. It all began when a friend introduced her to eBay. She began with 20 dollars and some bits of old furniture. Now her antiques company is making millions and she's worth fortune. 'It's a gold mine,' she said. 'I started out the red and eBay was like a miracle cure. If you've got something to sell, there's always somebody out there who's ready to buy it.'

PASSIVE REPORTING STRUCTURES

2 Rearrange the words in italics in the correct order.

1 Butch Cassidy and the Sundance Kid *been known have to are* two of the most successful bank robbers in the West.

_____

2 *that it been rumoured has* they met in prison where they were both serving sentences for horse theft.

_____

3 After a particularly daring robbery on a mining company *crossed they have to reported were* the border into Mexico. _____

4 However, *now is that it believed* they escaped to Argentina. _____

5 *that thought is it* they bought a ranch in Patagonia and started life afresh as honest cowboys.

_____

6 But then a nearby bank was robbed by two masked men *to said were have who spoken* in English. _____

7 Bounty hunters tracked down and shot two outlaws *be were to believed who* Butch and Sundance in a small town in Bolivia. _____

_____

3 Replace the words in italics with a passive reporting structure. Begin with the word in brackets.

1 *Many reports state that* the Sundance Kid never shot or killed anyone. (*it*)

_____

2 *There were rumours that* they were often accompanied by a woman. (*it*)

_____

3 She went by the name of Etta Place, though *many people believe this was a false name.* (*this*)

_____

4 *A lot of people said that they were* very polite and gentlemanly. (*they*)

_____

5 In Argentina, *there were rumours that they were* in trouble with the law. (*they*)

_____

6 *Some people have suggested that* they returned to a life of crime because they were bored. (*it*)

_____

TRANSLATION

4 Translate the text into your language.

Millions of items are bought and sold on eBay every day. Anything can be sold as long as it is not illegal. One of the biggest things that has ever been sold on the site was a World War II submarine. It was put up for auction by a small town in New England. A few tablespoons of water that had reportedly been left in a plastic cup after Elvis Presley had taken a drink from it were sold for $455.

12c | Scam

PHRASAL VERBS 2

1 Put the lines in the correct order

- [ ] **away** information like passwords or bank details. They use the details to apply for credit, shop online and generally **rip you**
- [ ] **up** all kinds of excuses in order to persuade you to **give**
- [ ] **away**. So why aren't we equally careful with our email? Millions of people have **fallen**
- [ ] **off**. And 9 times out of 10 the scammers **get away**
- [ ] **back** your money.
- [1] If a suspicious salesperson came to your door, you'd have no hesitation in **turning them**
- [ ] **for** bogus emails supposedly sent by banks or online shopping sites. The emails **make**
- [ ] **with it**. It is virtually impossible to get them to **hand**

2 Complete the sentences using an appropriate form of the phrasal verbs in bold in exercise 1.

1 They were _____ because they were not appropriately dressed.

2 The forgery was so good that literally thousands of people _____ it.

3 The thieves were forced to _____ the stolen goods.

4 The taxi driver _____ me _____, charging me twice the normal fare.

5 He _____ a story about how he had to get up early for work the next day.

6 Don't _____ your special access code to anyone outside the company.

CAUSATIVE

3 Complete the text with *to* + infinitive or the *-ed* form of the verbs in brackets.

Feeling lazy?

Get someone else (1) _____ (*do*) it for you – whatever it is! In today's service society, there's very little we have to do for ourselves any more. We can have our house (2) _____ (*clean*) by a cleaning service, we can have all our meals (3) _____ (*cook*) and (4) _____ (*deliver*) by a variety of different restaurants. We can get the hairdresser (5) _____ (*come*) to our home to style our hair and we can even ask a masseur to pop in to the office so we can have our feet (6) _____ (*massage*) as we work. We can get a personal shopper (7) _____ (*do*) all our shopping for us, and have it all (8)_____ (*bring*) to our front doors. And if we've got enough money, why not get a personal style consultant (9) _____ (*decide*) what we're going to wear every day?

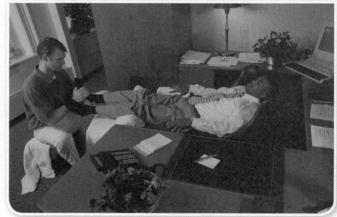

DICTATION

4 **35** Write the sentences that you hear.

1 _____.

2 _____.

3 _____.

4 _____.

12D | Dollar bill

GENERALIZING

1 Correct the mistakes in the sentences.

1 People worry more about money than their health, general speaking.
2 In the whole, pensioners are much better at keeping within their budgets than young people.
3 People carry less cash on them, on general, than they did ten years ago.
4 As the rule, supermarket shoppers prefer to pay by credit card than in cash.
5 For a most part, shops and restaurants are happy to accept all major credit cards.
6 People only use cash for minor purchases by or large, such as a cup of coffee, a newspaper or a bus ticket.

US & UK ENGLISH

2 Complete the crossword.

ACROSS
2 where you throw your rubbish if you live in the US (7,3)
5 the quickest way to get around in London (11)
6 where pedestrians walk along the side of roads in American towns and cities (8)
11 a large purple vegetable which is used in Mediterranean dishes (9)
12 if you're in the US and you need some water you could try turning this (6)

DOWN
1 this is where you go to refuel your car in the UK (6,7)
3 if you're in the US they've got long legs; if you're in the UK, you wear them under your trousers (5)
4 you wear this over your shirt in the US (4)

5 one way of getting to the other side of an American street (9)
7 see 5 down – this is what you'd use in the UK (6)
8 the UK version of 4 down (9)
9 this is what you would ask for at the end of your meal in a New York restaurant (5)
10 a game played with eleven players and a round ball (6)

3 Complete the dialogues with some of the words in the crossword in exercise 2.

1 **A:** Where's your dustbin?

   B: Sorry? Oh you mean, the _____ ! It's under the sink.

2 **A:** What's today's special?

   B: Egg plant with sun-dried tomatoes.

   A: Egg plant? What's that?

   B: Oh, sorry, I think you call it _____ .

3 **A:** Did you see the football on TV last night?

   B: Football? There wasn't any on last night.

   A: Sorry – I should have said _____ .

4 **A:** Excuse me. I'm having problems with the (4) _____ in our bathroom.

   B: I'm sorry, I don't understand.

   A: I can't seem to turn the hot water on.

5 **A:** Could we have the bill, please?

   B: Certainly, I'll bring you your (5) _____ , right away.

6 **A:** Hey, I love your new (6) _____ !

   B: What do you mean? Oh, you like my trousers – thanks!

TRANSLATION

4 Translate the joke into your language.

Question: How many tourists does it take to change a light bulb?

Answer: Fifteen. Five to figure out how much the bulb costs in the local currency, four to comment on 'how funny-looking' local lightbulbs are, three to hire a local person to change the bulb, two to take pictures, and one to buy postcards in case the pictures don't come out.

12 | Reading

1 Translate the words in bold in the dictionary extract into your language.

> **curse** /kɜːs/ verb *
>   **2** [T often passive] to use magic powers to make bad things happen to someone
> **curse** /kɜːs/ noun
>   **2** [C] a bad situation or event caused by someone's deliberate use of their magic powers: *the curse of the Pharaohs* – **put a curse on sb / sth** *He was sure someone had put a curse on his house.*
>   **2a** the words used for causing bad luck – opposite BLESSING
> **cursed** /kɜːst/ adj **1** affected in a negative way by a magic curse: *They were starting to believe that the house was cursed.*

2 Read the article on page 75 and choose the best summary.

1 Scientists have still not found an explanation of the Pharaoh's Curse.
2 The curse on Lord Caernarvon's family continues to this day.
3 *The Pharaoh's Curse* is an entertaining story.

3 Read the article again and choose the best answers.

1 Why did Lord Caernarvon think that his dreams had come true?
   a) Because he had his own racehorses.
   b) Because he had recovered from his car crash.
   c) Because he thought that Carter had discovered treasure.
   d) Because he was the owner of the gold of Tutankhamun.

2 What was special about Carter's discovery?
   a) It was the world's greatest archaeological discovery.
   b) The burial chamber was hidden behind a secret door.
   c) The Pharaoh's burial mask was wet.
   d) Tutankhamun was a boy-king.

3 Who encouraged people to believe in the curse of the Pharaoh?
   a) Egyptian archaeologists.
   b) Howard Carter.
   c) Popular newspapers.
   d) Sir Arthur Conan Doyle.

4 What happened to most of the people who went into the tomb?
   a) Nothing special.
   b) They breathed the mushroom spore.
   c) They died of mysterious illnesses.
   d) They lived in fear for the rest of their lives.

5 What does the writer think is the truth about Caernarvon's death?
   a) He was cursed by the Pharaoh.
   b) His death was caused by an insect.
   c) His murder will never be explained.
   d) Supernatural forces were probably responsible.

4 Match the words and phrases in the text 1–7 to the definitions a–g. The line numbers are in brackets.

1 was dripping with (34)
2 came to an untimely end (48)
3 had struck lucky (35)
4 desecrated (41)
5 dried up (53)
6 sparked the legend (57)
7 leave a lot to the imagination (78)

☐ a died before their time
☐ b do not provide all the necessary details
☐ c slowed down and stopped
☐ d spoiled a religious place
☐ e was covered in
☐ f was at the beginning of all the stories
☐ g were very fortunate

🔘 READ & LISTEN

5 🔘 **36** Listen to Reading 12 *The Pharaoh's Curse* on the CD and read the article again.

The Pharaoh's Curse

When George Herbert received a telegram telling him to come to Egypt immediately, he thought his dreams had come true. Herbert, better known as Lord Caernarvon, was a rich aristocrat, an owner of racehorses and a racing-car enthusiast. He was also a keen Egyptologist and for fifteen years he had been sponsoring the work of Howard Carter, an archaeologist who was searching for treasure in Egypt's Valley of the Kings. Carter had made an amazing discovery but would go no further without his sponsor. Archaeological work stopped until Caernarvon arrived in Cairo two weeks later. After four more days of digging, a door was uncovered in a tomb that belonged to the Pharaoh Tutankhamun. Carter was so excited that he spent the night at the tomb before he finally entered Tutankhamun's resting place the next day. With a candle in his hand, Carter said nothing for two or three minutes until the impatient Caernarvon asked him if he could see anything. 'Yes,' replied Carter, 'it is wonderful.'

Carter opens the tomb

The treasure that was spread out before them was the greatest that has ever been found. The burial chambers were stuffed with weapons, clothes, furniture and chariots, which took ten years to be catalogued. The body of Tutankhamun himself was found inside two coffins made of solid gold and the Pharaoh's burial mask, also of solid gold, was dripping with jewels. Carter and Caernarvon had struck lucky. But just five weeks after the opening of the tomb, Caernarvon became the first victim of the curse of the Pharaoh.

Doctors could not identify the mysterious illness that brought Caernarvon's life to a close. It was reported that mysterious forces had been released after Carter desecrated the tomb. The popular press jumped on the story and captured the public's imagination. One reporter claimed that a text near the entrance to the tomb read 'I will kill all who pass this door'. It was also reported that the lights in Cairo had gone out at the moment of Caernarvon's death. Within ten years, six more people who had been present at the opening of the tomb had come to an untimely end. Where would the curse of the Pharaoh strike next?

Sir Arthur Conan Doyle, creator of Sherlock Holmes, was convinced that the Pharaoh's tomb contained a deadly mushroom spore and that more deaths would follow. But surprisingly, the number of victims dried up. Later studies showed that the average age of death of those who had gone into the tomb was relatively low. Many of Carter's team lived well into old age, and the death that sparked the legend of the curse turned out to be not so mysterious after all. In actual fact, Caernarvon, who had never fully recovered his health following a car crash, was killed by a mosquito bite which became infected. This, remember, was at a time before antibiotics, and the power supply in Cairo was very irregular.

But the curse of the Pharaoh and the tales of walking mummies continue to live today. Despite substantial evidence to the contrary, it seems that there are many people who are ready to believe that dark, supernatural forces are behind the deaths of Caernarvon and others. Could it have been the work of an evil spirit? Or was it radiation from radioactive rocks in the tomb? Had the ancient Egyptians made contact with alien visitors and developed sophisticated technology? Was Tutankhamun himself the victim of a cold-blooded murder? The theories are fun, but they leave a lot to the imagination, and, sadly, are only the stuff of Hollywood.

Writing at Upper Intermediate level

You may be wondering why we've included more writing at this level of *Straightforward*. The reason for this is because writing often becomes so much more important at Upper Intermediate level – when you may need to write English for school project work, for business or to take examinations.

Writing is often challenging in another language and we can sometimes feel more pressure. It's important to get it right – if we *say* something wrong in another language people forget it quickly, but when we write, people can be less forgiving and, as it's recorded in print, they may read it again and again!

In order for you to become a good writer of English, it's important to remember a few golden rules:

- Don't hurry – give yourself lots of time. Always plan your writing before you start. It can be helpful to read the question you need to answer and then go away and 'chew it over' during the day. This may help to make your ideas clear.
- Sit down and plan the structure of your writing. The structure will make it easier for the reader to follow your thoughts and enjoy your writing. Try to think of something original to say about the topic so that your reader is interested and motivated to read more.
- When you begin writing, don't make your sentences too long. In some languages it's considered good style to use very long and grammatically complex sentences. This is not usually the case in English.
- Try to use basic words less at Upper Intermediate level. For example, instead of *and*, try to use words and expressions such as *moreover* and *as well as*; instead of *but*, use *however* and *despite*.
- Remember to use common phrases traditionally used for different types of writing. See page 77 to help you with this. This will make your writing more sophisticated and natural.
- Always leave time to check your written work. If you feel a bit unsure about it, why not do one section early and show it to your teacher? It might be helpful to get some feedback before you write the whole composition.
- Finally, enjoy writing! It's fun to write, and it can become just as much fun in another language, once you've understood the conventions of that language.

Workbook writing lessons

There are six writing units in this Workbook. Each unit consists of two pages (A & B) which practise and build on the writing lessons in the Student's Book.

Page A provides **additional practice of the language focus points** presented in the Student's Book. Use these pages alongside the Student's Book writing lessons.

Page B provides **a structured writing 'lesson', building up to a writing task**. These pages tie in with the topics of the even numbered units in the Student's Book. Sample answers for these writing tasks are provided in the answer key (pages i–xvi).

Student's Book		Workbook
Unit 1	A job application	1A Applying for a job (1)
Unit 2		1B Applying for a job (2)
Unit 3	A composition	2A Writing a composition (1)
Unit 4		2B Writing a composition (2)
Unit 5	A review	3A Writing a review (1)
Unit 6		3B Writing a review (2)
Unit 7	An email to a friend	4A Wrtiing to a friend (1)
Unit 8		4B Wrtiing to a friend (2)
Unit 9	A story	5A Writing a story (1)
Unit 10		5B Writing a story (2)
Unit 11	A report	6A Writing a report (1)
Unit 12		6B Writing a report (2)

I'VE GOT ALL THE WORDS I NEED FOR MY NOVEL, IT'S JUST A CASE OF PUTTING THEM IN THE RIGHT ORDER NOW!

Useful language to improve your writing

Narrative language

At first … .
At the beginning … .
Initially … .
To begin with … .
After a while … .
Later on … .
Afterwards … .
Subsequently … .
Eventually … .
In the end … .
Finally … .

Writing a covering letter

I am writing in response/reply to your advertisement.
I understand you are currently looking for … .
I would like to apply for the position of … .
I am interested in gaining experience in … .
I have enclosed/attached my CV and the names of two referees.
I am available for interview/to begin work at your convenience.
Please do not hesitate to contact me if you require further information.
I look forward to hearing from you.
Thank you for your time and consideration.

Expressing an opinion

It could be argued that … .
It is fair to say that … .
It is generally recognized … .
It is reasonable to say … .
It seems to me … .
Many people feel … .
Most people would agree … .
There is no doubt that … .

Describing a film/TV show/series

The show/film is named after/based on … .
The series/film centres on … .
It follows the lives of … .
It tells the story of … ./It paints a very accurate picture of … .
The star of the show/film is … ./It stars … .
The role of … is played by … .
His performance is worthy of an Oscar/Emmy.
What I liked most/least about it was … .
Critics praise it for … .

Informal greetings (emails, notes, postcards)

Hi/Hello! How are you doing?
Thanks for your email/letter.
Sorry I haven't written for ages/so long.
It's/was great to hear from you!
Sorry I missed your call.
This is just a quick note to say … .
Speak to you later.
Bye for now. Speak soon.
All the best and love to the family.
Say hi to everyone from me.
Love from everybody here.
Keep in touch.

Invitations
Informal

Do you feel like going out tonight?
How about coming with us?
Do you fancy doing something later?
What about coming round to my place?
Would you like to come with us?
We were wondering if you'd like to come with us.

Formal

It gives us great pleasure to invite you to … .
We would be delighted/pleased if you could join us.
Mr & Mrs X request the pleasure of your company at … .

Writing a report
Introduction

The purpose of this report is to … .
The report will discuss/analyze/describe … .
The following report examines/reviews/considers … .
The report is divided into three parts.

Conclusion/recommendations

I would like to suggest/recommend that … .
Taking everything into consideration … .
On balance, I think that … .
To sum up, I suggest we … .
In conclusion, my own view is that … .

Writing the minutes for a meeting

Here is a summary of the decisions taken and the action agreed on … .
X opened the meeting by … .
It was agreed that … .
After some discussion, it was eventually decided that … .
X has agreed to/volunteered to … .
Y presented the results/the options … .
The next meeting will be held on … .

LANGUAGE FOCUS

1 Find and underline ten unnecessary capital letters in the CV extracts.

1

> I translated over 2,000 Recipes from Spanish to English for a web-based recipe book, *La Cocina Española*. The Job involved liaising with my co-writer, Jane Goode and the Editors responsible for the Project.

2

> I am a highly motivated and enthusiastic Graphic Design Student. I am looking for an initial placement in a dynamic work environment.

3

> rock-climbing: I was an active member of the outdoor pursuit club at School and have been interested in Rock Climbing ever since.

2 Match the extracts 1–3 in exercise 1 to one of the CV sections.

Personal profile
Education
Work experience
Skills
Interests
References

3 Choose the correct spelling, a, b or c.

1 a) profesional b) professional c) proffessional
2 a) personal b) personel c) personnal
3 a) knowlege b) knowlegde c) knowledge
4 a) essential b) esential c) essentiel
5 a) expereince b) experiense c) experience
6 a) sucessful b) successful c) succesful
7 a) volontary b) voluntery c) voluntary
8 a) responsibilities b) responsabilities c) responsibilitys
9 a) referrees b) referres c) referees

4 Complete the text with the correctly-spelt words from exercise 3.

> A (1) _____ CV will include information about your work (2) _____, your (3) _____ qualifications and your (4) _____ qualities. Remember to include all relevant jobs, including (5) _____ work and add a short description of the duties and (6) _____ involved. It is also (7) _____ that you include information about your (8) _____ of languages and computing skills. Last, but not least, remember to include the names and contact details of two (9) _____.

5 Complete the sentences 1–6 with the phrases a–f.

A
1 I **am experienced**
2 I particularly enjoy **helping**
3 My **duties**
4 **I am looking**
5 I **was an active**
6 I worked as a volunteer **at**

B
☐ a **member of** the university's film society. _____
☐ b **included** liaising between parents and school authorities. _____
☐ c **in** restaurant work and outside catering. _____
☐ d **other people with their work.** _____
☐ e **first** and was then given a job as a part-time guide. _____
☐ f **for** a job in the retail industry. _____

6 Match the sentences in exercise 5 to the jobs in the box.

> chef   film critic   museum curator
> personal assistant   shop assistant   teacher

7 Replace the phrases in bold in exercise 5 with one of the expressions 1–6.

1 took an active part in
2 job involved
3 have experience of
4 supporting the work of others
5 initially
6 my aim is to find

1B | Writing Applying for a job (2)

READING

1 Look at the covering letter and answer these questions.

1 What kind of job is Mark looking for?
2 Has he done this kind of job before?

Dear Mr Wright,

I understand from an article on your website that you are looking for volunteers to help out at the animal rescue shelter in Newham. I am writing to enquire whether you have any vacancies for the months of June and July, as I will be staying with friends in the area during that period. I am currently studying Journalism at Cardiff University and I am looking for an opportunity to work in the voluntary sector with a view to publishing an article about my experience. Although I have not worked at an animal shelter before, I am an animal lover. I have had experience of looking after a variety of pets and farmyard animals, including dogs, cats, horses, sheep and goats. I am familiar with your organization and greatly admire the work you do. I would really like to help in whatever way I can. If I could be of use in your Press Department, this would be a welcome bonus.

I have included a copy of my CV. I will try to contact you within the week to arrange an interview. Thank you for your time and consideration.

Yours sincerely,

Mark Goodsworth

---

2 Look at the covering letter again and decide if these statements are true (T) or false (F).

1 Mark is writing in response to a job advert. ___

2 He has never worked for an animal shelter. ___

3 He is looking for a job for the summer holidays. ___

4 He doesn't know much about the organization. ___

5 He's going to call or write again in a few days' time. ___

6 He's going to send a copy of his CV by post. ___

LANGUAGE FOCUS

1 Complete the phrases 1–8 with the phrases a–h.

A
1 I am writing to
2 I am looking for
3 I am currently
4 I have included

5 I will try to contact you within the week to
6 Thank you for
7 I am familiar with your organization and
8 I have had experience of

B
- [ ] a an opportunity to work in the voluntary sector.
- [ ] b arrange an interview.
- [ ] c enquire whether you have any vacancies for July.
- [ ] d greatly admire the work you do.
- [ ] e looking after a variety of pets and animals.
- [ ] f studying Journalism at Cardiff University.
- [ ] g your time and consideration.
- [ ] h a copy of my CV.

2 Match sentences from exercise 1 to the points a–f in the notes.

> **How to write a covering letter**
> Whether you are answering a job advert or sending your CV to a potential employer you should always write an accompanying cover letter. The letter should include the following points:
> **Paragraph 1**
> a   Introduce yourself
> b   Explain your reason for writing
> **Paragraph 2**
> c   Describe your experience
> d   Explain why you are interested in the organization
> **Paragraph 3**
> e   Promise to follow up on your application
> f   Thank the reader for considering your application

WRITING

1 Choose one of the organizations below. Write a covering letter enquiring about the possibility of work during the next holidays. Remember to follow the advice given in Language focus exercise 2.

SUMMER WORK
Join the crew of the Sea Heaven on its annual summer cruise around the Pacific. Many positions available: bar, restaurant, activities organizer, cleaning, baby-sitting service, etc. Good rates of pay. Send CV to Heaven Cruises, P.O. Box 666, Grand Cayman

HOTEL STAFFING SOLUTIONS INC
We are currently looking for staff to fill temporary positions in hotels in 5 continents. Vacancies for all types of work. Free training, flights and insurance. Tax free. Fax CV and cover letter NOW to: HSS Inc + 371 22 060606 (ref. XP8)

2A | Writing A composition (1)

LANGUAGE FOCUS

1 Put the paragraphs in the correct order.

☐ _____ Skirt-like garments are worn by men all over the world, either as part of their national dress or as an everyday alternative to trousers. The Greeks and Albanians wear the *fustanella* – a pleated white skirt – as part of their traditional costume. Many men in Southern India wear *dhotis* – checked cotton sarongs – both for work and leisure. In the Himalayan Kingdom of Bhutan all men wear a knee-length robe called a *gho*.

☐ _____ The Irish have their own version of the kilt, too, as do the Welsh, and many Celtic émigrés wear kilts as a symbol of their heritage. Kilts are also fast becoming a fashion item. Celebrities (footballers, pop singers, film stars) are increasingly being photographed in variations on the traditional kilt. A Seattle-based company has launched the *utilikilt*, a modern take on the traditional kilt, designed for day-to-day use.

☐ _____ Kilt historians suggest that the kilt may have originated in Norway and was subsequently introduced to Scotland by the Vikings. Whatever the truth of its origins, there is no doubt that a man in a kilt is synonymous with Scottishness. Although more than 80% of Scotsmen do not actually own a kilt, most will, at some time, hire one for a formal occasion, be it for weddings, football matches or to attend the Highland Games.

2 Insert the topic sentences a–c at the begining of the paragraphs in exercise 1.

a Kilts are not exclusive to Scotland – there are kilts from other countries too.
b The kilt is probably the most well-known symbol of Scotland.
c Kilts are not the only alternative to trousers for men.

3 Complete the sentences with a phrase in the box.

complete without	favourite icons
not the only	of which less than
synonymous with	the best known of

☐ 1 The double-decker bus is _____ London.

☐ 2 Cuddly koala bears are another of Australia's _____.

☐ 3 Kangaroos are probably _____ all Australian animals.

☐ 4 No image of London transport is _____ the inclusion of a black cab.

☐ 5 The large red bus is _____ form of transport associated with the capital city.

☐ 6 Australia is an enormous country, _____ 10% is inhabited.

4 Match the topic sentences in exercise 3 to the composition titles, a or b. Then order the sentences 1–6 above, as they would appear in the composition.

a Images of the Capital _____
b Australian wildlife _____

5 Choose the correct word to complete the sentences.

1 It could be *argued / agree* that it has some of the most beautiful beaches in the world.
2 It is fair to *say / doubt* that it has never been famous for its food.
3 It is *general / generally* recognized that it produces the finest wines in the region.
4 It is *reasonable / reasonably* to say that it is one of the world's richest countries.
5 It *seems / feels* to me that it is often misrepresented in the world press.
6 Many people *seem / feel* that its image needs updating.
7 Most people would *argued / agree* that it is a great holiday destination
8 There is no *say / doubt* that its historic importance is greatly undervalued.

6 Which of the sentences in exercise 5 are true for your country?

2B Writing A composition (2)

READING

1 Read the composition and put the paragraphs in the correct order.

☐ He began stealing cattle to provide for his family and, before long, he and his gang were on the run. They robbed banks and shared the money with friends and family. In no time, Ned had gained himself a reputation as an Australian Robin Hood.

Ned Kelly: an Australian hero

☐ But after the gang killed three police officers in a shoot out, he also gained a reputation as a police killer. He and his gang were finally captured in Glenrowan, a small town in Victoria. Three gang members were killed. Ned was arrested and charged with murder. He was hanged in 1880 at 25 years of age.

☐ The outlaw, Ned Kelly, is one of Australia's greatest folk heroes. But he is also a source of great debate. Was he a working-class hero, or a criminal who robbed and killed?

☐ A year later, an enquiry into the Glenrowan siege resulted in the dismissal of several police officers. The town of Glenrowan has become synonymous with the Kelly legend and, every ten years, a re-enactment is held of the gang's historic last stand.

☐ From a young age, Ned was in trouble with the law. At the age of sixteen, he was wrongfully imprisoned for stealing a horse and from then on, he was convinced that the police were persecuting him and his family.

2 Read the composition again and number the events 1–6 in the correct order.

☐ Ned was hanged.
☐ Police officers lost their jobs.
☐ The Kelly gang started robbing banks.
☐ *1* Ned was accused of stealing a horse.
☐ Three policemen were killed.
☐ Glenrowan became famous.

LANGUAGE FOCUS

1 Complete the text with the time expressions in the box.

at 38 years of age	At the age of eleven
before long	Eleven years later
from a young age	From then on

PHOOLAN DEVI

A Phoolan Devi, otherwise known as the Bandit Queen, fought for the rights of low-caste women in India, first as the leader of a gang of bandits and later as a Member of Parliament.

B Phoolan, born into a poor fishing family, rebelled against her fate (1) _____.
(2) _____ she was sold into marriage, but she stood up to her husband's abuse and was thrown out of his house. It is thought that she was then kidnapped by a gang of bandits and (3) _____ she had become one of them. When a group of upper-caste villagers killed her bandit lover, Phoolan formed her own gang. (4) _____, she took revenge on the landowners who made life so difficult for the poor villagers.

C For ten years she led raids to save child brides from early marriages and stole from the upper caste landowners. She eventually surrendered to the police and was sent to prison. (5) _____ she was released and stood for Parliament. There, she continued her fight for women's rights until, (6) _____, she was shot and killed outside her home in New Delhi.

2 Look at the text in exercise 1 and complete the paragraph summaries with the words in the box.

| early | famous | grew | how | summary |
| why | brief | | | |

A a (1) _____ explanation of (2) _____ the person is (3) _____

B a (4) _____ of the person's (5) _____ life

C a description of (6) _____ the legend (7) _____

WRITING

1 Use the paragraph summaries in Language focus exercise 2 to write a composition about a hero from your country.

3A | Writing A review (1)

LANGUAGE FOCUS

1 Complete the review with the correct prepositions.

This classic TV mini series was first released (a) _____ 1996, but it is still a top ten favourite. This is arguably the best screen adaptation (b) _____ Jane Austen's much-loved novel. Colin Firth, in the role (c) _____ Darcy, is masterful. The chemistry between him and Elizabeth Bennet (played (d) _____ Jennifer Ehle) really brings the story to life. The action is set (e) _____ a series of beautiful stately homes, the cast are dressed (f) _____ meticulous period costume, and the choreography and music all add up to a truly great experience.

2 Complete the review with the missing words.

The film (1) a_____ of *Bridget Jones's Diary* is a total success. It tells the (2) s_____ of Helen Fielding's best-selling novel of the same name and manages to convey the same sense of humour and romance as the original. Renée Zellweger is totally (3) c_____ as paranoid 30-something Bridget, and the role of Mark Darcy is played to (4) p_____ by Colin Firth. Personally, I think his performance is (5) w_____ of an Oscar! And anyone who saw *Pride and Prejudice* (the TV mini-series that (6) s_____ Colin Firth as the original Mr Darcy) is sure to agree.

3 Complete the text with the phrases in the box.

in the lead role   It tells the story   Its plot is
Most of the action   which featured
The best moment in the whole movie
The cast has no stars   the part

Attack of the Killer Tomatoes has been called one of the cheapest and worst science fiction movies of all time. (1) _____ of a group of scientists who save the world from the threat of mutant tomatoes that have turned violent. (2) _____ is an accidental helicopter crash, but this unfortunate pilot error obviously ate up the entire budget for special effects. (3) _____ clearly takes place in a studio and the killer tomatoes are less than frightening when you can see their wheels. (4) _____ and their involvement in *Killer Tomatoes* did not help their careers. David Miller looks uncomfortable (5) _____ and you have to wonder why he accepted (6) _____. Ten years after the film's release, a sequel, *Return of the Killer Tomatoes*, (7) _____ a young George Clooney, was made. (8) _____ basically the same as the original.

4 Look at the pictures. Write a short description of the plot of *Attack of the Killer Tomatoes* using the simple present.

3B | Writing A review (2)

READING

1 Read the review of a TV series and decide whether it is mainly positive or negative.

The West Wing

The West Wing, a TV drama series which centres on the White House, is one of the most popular TV shows in the US. It is watched by more than fifteen million viewers each week and it has won a record number of Emmy awards.

The show follows the life of fictional Democrat president, Jed Bartlet, and his team, during their eight years in office. Jed Bartlet (played by Martin Sheen) is undoubtedly the star of the show. The president's role was fairly unimportant in the first few shows but audience reactions soon prompted the programme makers to bring him centre-stage.

The show is named after the West Wing of the White House, the location of the president's Oval Office and the offices of his senior staff. Real-life politicians follow the show closely and say it paints a very accurate picture of how the US government actually works. Educationalists praise the show, saying that it helps people understand the complex workings of government, while TV critics praise it for the quality of its dialogue and story lines.

2 Read the review again. Put the topics in the order in which they are mentioned.

- ☐ the main character
- ☐ the name
- ☐ what people say about it
- ☐ the setting
- ☐ the story and the characters
- ☐ the number of people who watch it

LANGUAGE FOCUS

1 Complete the review with the phrases a–f.

a   The show is named …
b   The series centres …
c   It follows …
d   it paints a very accurate picture …
e   the star of the show is …
f   TV critics praise it …

The Office must be the number one TV comedy series ever!
(1) _____ on a paper company in Slough and
(2) _____ the day-to-day lives of the office workers in the style of a documentary. (3) _____ after the location of all the scenes – the various offices and meetings rooms of the paper company.

There is no doubt that (4) _____ David Brent, played by comic genius Ricky Gervais. His performance is magnificent, as are those of all the cast. Office workers around the world will all agree that (5) _____ of the world of office politics, and (6) _____ for its hilarious dialogue and perfect timing.

2 Complete the sentence frames in exercise 1 so that they are true for a TV series you know.

WRITING

1 Write a review of a popular series on TV in your country. Remember to include information about the setting, the storyline and the characters and to explain why it is so popular.

LANGUAGE FOCUS

1 Put the lines in the correct order for an email message.

☐ We really must get together and catch up sometime soon.

☐ Maybe we can meet up then.

☐ Lots of love, T.

☐ I'm sorry I was out when you phoned.

☐ I can't believe it's been three months since we last spoke. So much has happened!

☐ Speak to you later today,

☐ I'll phone you later today when I know the dates for sure.

☐ I'm coming down to London next week for a business meeting.

☐ Right, got to go now, the boss is looking over my shoulder!

☐1 Hi Jane, thanks for your message.

2 Compete the sentences with a word in the box.

again	call	doing	last	nice	now
quick	too				

1 Hello, how are you _____?

2 Thanks for your email. It was so _____ to hear from you!

3 Just a _____ note to say we had a really good time last night.

4 OK. 8 o'clock suits me, _____.

5 Anyway, sorry _____ I can't come. I hope you have a great time!

6 I'll _____ you at the weekend to see how things are going.

7 One _____ thing. Can you get some bread in on the way home? Thx!

8 Bye for _____. Speak soon.

3 Reorder the words in italics to form invitations.

1 *fancy you going do* to the cinema tonight? That new French film's on. _____

2 Hi, *invite you writing to I'm to* a surprise party for Debby's 30th birthday.

_____

3 Mr and Mrs Bob Carl *company of pleasure your the request* at their daughter's graduation ceremony.

_____

4 Sorry, I can't make the party tonight. *to place coming what round my about* tomorrow for something to eat? _____

5 We're going to the beach for the weekend. *if wondering we like were would you to* come with us.

_____

6 *us be pleased you could join we very would if* to celebrate the launch of our new high street store.

_____

4 Match the expressions a–f to the answers in exercise 3.

☐ a do you feel like going …

☐ b how about coming here …

☐ c it gives us great pleasure to invite you …

☐ d will you be able to come to … ?

☐ e would be delighted if you could join them …

☐ f would you like to …

5 Complete four short emails. Choose language that is appropriately formal or informal.

1 to a close friend – you want to do something together this evening

> Jo
>
> Are you doing anything this evening?

2 to a group of friends telling them some good news

> Hi everyone!
>
> Sorry for sending a circular email, but I'm incredibly busy at the moment.

3 to a business partner arranging a meeting

> Dear Mr Jones
>
> I am writing to you further to our discussion earlier this week.

4 to a family friend in response to an invitation

> Dear Alex
>
> Many thanks for your email.

4B | Writing Writing to a friend (2)

READING

1 Match the pictures to the messages.

- [ ] a a greetings card
- [ ] b a postcard
- [ ] c a note
- [ ] d an e-greeting

2 Match the texts 1–4 to the messages a–d in exercise 1.

- [ ] 1
  > Congratulations! He looks absolutely gorgeous, just like his dad! :)
  >
  > Lots of love from the four of us, Si.

- [ ] 2
  > So sorry to hear about the accident. I'm glad you're on the mend. Love from everybody here, Amanda.

- [ ] 3
  > Here we are, on the beach at last. The sun and the swimming is really helping my back! Hoping to be back on full form next week!
  >
  > Say hi to everyone at work,
  >
  > Jon

- [ ] 4
  > Gone to the dentist. See you at about 6pm. T.

LANGUAGE FOCUS

1 Compare the message to the shorter version in Reading exercise 2. Cross out all the unnecessary words.

> I've gone to my appointment with the dentist. It won't take long. I'll see you when I get back. I should be back at about 6 at the latest. Love, Tracy.

2 Rewrite these messages, making them as brief as possible.

A
> Sam called to say he's in town. I've gone to meet him at the pub. We'll be there until about 9pm I imagine. Why don't you come and join us when you get home?

B
> Thank you so much for your e-greeting. We're back home now from the hospital. It's really nice to be at home with little baby Huw. He's a really good baby. He's eating and sleeping well and we just can't take our eyes off him!

C
> Thank you very much indeed for your kind card. It was nice to know that you're all thinking of me! The doctors say that things are going very well and I should be home by the end of next week. Please say hello to everyone at the office from me. All the best, Kay.

D
> Thank you for the beautiful postcard. I'm very glad to hear your back's getting better. We're all looking forward to seeing you back at work again next week, J! We all hope you enjoy the rest of your holiday. We'll see you soon, all the best, Rod.

3 Match the replies A–D above to the messages 1–4 in Reading exercise 2.

WRITING

1 Write replies to the following messages. Remember to keep them as brief as possible.

1
> Home at 8. Fancy eating out? R x

2
> Won't be able to make the football tonight. I've done something to my knee – again! ☹. May have to go to the doctor's this time!
>
> Tim

3
> Hi everybody, exciting news: Nina's pregnant! The baby's due in September.

4
> Have a great holiday. Remember to send a postcard!

5A | Writing A story (1)

LANGUAGE FOCUS

1 Replace the words in italics 1–5 with a word in the box.

he	him	she	her	they	them	their

Teenage hero saves family

15-year-old Travis Jude saved housewife Anne Shipley and (1) *Anne's* three small children aged two, five and seven from certain death on Saturday night. It was two o'clock in the morning. Travis was walking home from the pub when (2) *Travis* heard someone shouting for help. (3) *Travis* looked up and saw the Shipley house in flames. Anne was standing at a first floor window with (4) *Anne's* youngest boy, James, in (5) *Anne's* arms. Travis didn't think twice. (6) *Travis* ran into the house and came out carrying the older kids, Suzy (aged five) and Danny (aged seven). (7) *Suzy and Danny* were scared, but unhurt. Travis then turned around and went back into the burning house a second time. Two minutes later (8) *Travis* came out again, this time Anne and baby James were with (9) *Travis* and the family were all safely reunited in (10) *the family's* garden. The fire brigade turned up half an hour later. It took (11) *the fire brigade* four hours to put the fire out. (12) *The firemen* explained that the fire was caused by an electrical fault in the kitchen.

2 Underline the five expressions used to describe the main characters in the story.

Three students were recovering last night after spending a night at sea in sub-zero temperatures. The youngsters had gone out for a short trip along the coast on Sunday afternoon, wearing only jeans and light jackets. Their boat ran out of petrol after about half an hour and strong currents carried the unlucky trio over two miles away from the coast.

The boys' disappearance was reported to the authorities later that evening when they failed to turn up for a friend's birthday party. The wind was too strong for **them** to send out a helicopter that night and **they** had to wait until the next morning before they could start their search. **They** finally found the boat at two o'clock in the afternoon, exactly 24 hours after the three friends had first set out.

3 Choose three expressions from the list a–f that can replace the words in bold in the story in exercise 2.

a   the rescue team
b   the boys' friends
c   the families of the three boys
d   the helicopter crew
e   the emergency services
f   local newspaper reporters

4 Match each quotation to one of the people a–f in exercise 3.

1   we were so happy when we heard they'd been found – the coastguard did a fantastic job

c the families of the three boys

2   you should always make sure you've got a full tank of fuel before you set out on a boat trip – no matter how short _____

3   how did you feel when you realized you were drifting out to sea? _____

4   when they didn't turn up for the party, we phoned the coastguard _____

5   when we found them, they were cold and frightened

_____

6   it was hard work flying in those conditions – but it's all part of the job _____

5 Punctuate the quotations in exercise 4.

1   'We were so happy when we heard they'd been found,' said the families of the three boys.

2   '_____'.

3   '_____'.

4   '_____'.

5   '_____'.

6   '_____'.

5B | Writing A story (2)

READING

1 Match the stories A–C to the titles 1–3.

☐ 1 Running late
☐ 2 A guilty note
☐ 3 A kind word

A

A man returned from shopping to find his car had been badly dented. As he walked up to the car he saw a note had been left on his windscreen. Laughing at himself for doubting the honesty of the average person, he pulled the note away and read it.

B

A man was waiting to pay at the supermarket when he noticed an elderly lady staring at him. He asked her if something was wrong. The lady began to cry and explained that he looked like her son, who had died in a car crash. She asked him if he'd mind saying 'goodbye, mom' to her when she waved to him. Because he felt sorry for her, he agreed to do it.

C

A man was on his way to a date one night when he realized he'd got on the wrong train. This was the express that would only slow down, but not stop, at his station. He didn't want to be late so when the train arrived at his station, he jumped out.

2 Find the ending for each story in exercise 1.

☐ 1 When it was his turn to pay, his bill was enormous. The cashier explained that his mother had said he'd pay for her groceries. The cashier, who had heard him say goodbye to the old lady, ignored his protests.
☐ 2 It said: 'The people watching me think I'm leaving my name and address, but I'm not.'
☐ 3 A conductor grabbed his jacket and pulled him back onto the train the conductor said youre lucky i saw you dont you know this train doesnt stop here

LANGUAGE FOCUS

1 Punctuate the end of the third story (C) in the Reading section.

2 Combine the sentences with the word or words in brackets.

1 A man returned from shopping. He saw his car had been badly dented. (*to find*)
2 He walked up to his car. He saw a note that had been left on his windscreen. (*as*)
3 A man was waiting to pay at the supermarket. He noticed an elderly lady staring at him. (*when*)
4 He felt sorry for her. He agreed to do it. (*because*)
5 He didn't want to be late. When the train arrived at his station, he jumped out. (*so*)
6 The cashier had heard him say goodbye to the old woman. She ignored his protests. (*who*)

Check your answers in the reading texts.

WRITING

1 Complete the story with the words in brackets.

An elderly lady had finished her shopping and went back to her car in the car park.
1 (*see   four men   drive away   her car*)

She saw four men driving away in her car.

She dropped her bags, drew out a handgun, and screamed, 'I have a gun, and I know how to use it! Get out of the car!'
2 (*four men   get out   run away*)

_____.

The lady put her bags in the back of the car and got into the driver's seat.
3 (*shaken   start car   key not fit*)

_____.

A few minutes later she found her own car parked four or five spaces farther down.
4 (*drive   police station   report story*)

_____.

The policeman laughed when he heard her story. He pointed to the other end of the counter.
5 (*four men   car stolen   lady handgun*)

_____.

6A | Writing A report (1)

LANGUAGE FOCUS

1 Complete the report extracts A–C and D–F with the words in the boxes.

Beginning a report

| following | follows | provide | purpose |
| requested | suitability | view | |

A The (1) _____ of this report is to (2) _____ information about the recently opened Powys Outdoor Sports Centre with a (3) _____ to adding it to our list of optional excursions.

B The report which (4) _____ examines the (5) _____ of Newtown Industrial Park as a location for our new production unit.

C As (6) _____ at the last management meeting, the (7) _____ report provides further details about the accommodation available at Gold Park.

Closing a report

| suggest | suitable | sum | view | consideration |

D Taking everything into (8) _____, the site would not seem to be (9) _____ for our specific business needs.

E My own (10) _____ is that the complex would be a valuable addition to our current brochure.

F To (11) _____ up, I (12) _____ we await developments before including this centre on our social activities programme.

2 Match the extracts A–F to one of the report types, 1, 2 or 3.

1   A report on a new tourist attraction
2   A report on possible new business premises
3   A report on a new hotel complex

3 Put the lines in the correct order.

- [ ] the **neighbouring** towns of Padstow and
- [ ] perfectly **located** at an equal distance from
- [ ] equipped and very comfortable and they
- [ ] **overlooking** the Cornish coastline. It is
- [ ] sunsets over the wide, sandy beach below.
- [ ] all **offer** superb views of the **spectacular**
- [ ] **drive** away. The hotel rooms are well-
- [ ] Newquay, both a short fifteen minute
- [1] The Seagull Hotel stands on a hill

4 Replace the words in bold in the text in exercise 3 with a word or phrase in the box.

| breathtaking | looking out over | situated | nearby |
| car journey | provide | | |

5 Complete the sentences with *although*, *despite* or *however*.

1   _____ the menu at the Seagull Hotel is limited, the food is always freshly cooked and of a very high standard.

2   The Hotel has no bar and there are no pubs nearby. _____, both Padstow and Torquay have great night life at the weekend.

3   _____ its size, I have no hesitation in recommending the Seagull Hotel for our annual reunion.

4   _____, if we decide not to stay at the Seagull, I would recommend the Royale, which is bigger and located in the centre of town.

5   It is very friendly and welcoming, _____ being part of a large chain.

6   _____ I prefer the idea of staying at The Seagull, I'm sure a stay at the Royale would be equally successful.

6 Use the report form to give details about a hotel in your town or area.

Accommodation report: local hotels

The purpose of this report is to provide basic information about (*name of the hotel*) ....

1 Location

It is situated _____.

2 The facilities

The hotel offers _____.

3 Recommendation

In conclusion, I recommend _____.

READING

1 Read this report of a meeting held by the Blackwater Dive Club and answer the questions.

1 Why was the meeting called?
2 What decisions were taken at the meeting?

Blackwater Dive Club
Meeting: Cocos Island trip
Wednesday 26th 8.30

Thanks to everyone for turning up to last night's meeting. I think you'll agree it was very productive. Here is a summary of the decisions taken and the action agreed on.

Harriet opened the meeting by presenting the travel options available. We all agreed that we would stay in San José for two nights before boarding the dive boat. As you know, there is no accommodation on Cocos Island, so we will be staying on the boat until we get back to San José.

After some discussion, we decided that we would charter a boat for five days (four nights) from the 18th to the 22nd. Some members suggested spending more time on the boat and sailing back to San José on the day of our return flight. But in the end we opted for another two-night stay on the way back.

Harriet has agreed to book the boat, Jo has volunteered to find out about hotels and guesthouses in San José and Ken is going to book the flights as he can get us a 20% discount.

The next meeting will be on Wednesday 3rd at 8.30 to discuss travel arrangements to and from the airport. Please bring any information you can about cheap transfer options.

---

2 Read the report again and complete the table.

Decisions made	Action to be taken	Person responsible
Four nights in San José	(1) _____	Jo
(2) _____	Charter boat	(3) _____
Flights from Heathrow to San José	(4) _____	(5) _____
Travel to/ from airport	(6) _____	Everyone!

LANGUAGE FOCUS

1 Underline all the reporting verbs in the report and add the missing letters to the words 1–6.

1 a _ _ _ e   4 o _ t
2 d _ _ _ _ e   5 s _ _ _ _ _ t
3 d _ _ _ _ _ s   6 v _ _ _ _ _ _ _ r

2 Complete the text with an appropriate form of the verb on the right.

Harriet presented two options for travel arrangements to the airport. After much (1) _____ and initial (2) _____ it was eventually (3) _____ to hire a minibus to take us to and from the airport and Dave's (4) _____ of asking his cousin to drive the bus was (5) _____ on unanimously. Jo (6) _____ to make sandwiches for the outward journey.	discuss disagree decide suggest agree volunteer

WRITING

1 Use the notes to write a report of the Blackwater Dive Club's first meeting after they got back from their trip.

Points raised	Who by
Great trip – despite airport strike. Agreed	Harriet
Write letter of complaint to local newspaper about strike. Agreed in part	Dave Dave to write it
Thank-you card & present (what?) for the crew of the 'Caribbean Star'.	Jo & Ken
Digital photo album.	Harriet
Copies to be made for all club members too.	Dave Dave to do
Next meeting: screening of Cocos Island DVD.	Ken

Anna Karenina

The People in This Story

Countess Vronskaya

Vronsky

Anna Karenina

Alexei Karenin

Stiva Oblonsky

Dolly Oblonsky

Annie

Sasha Karenin

Constantine Levin

Kitty Oblonsky

Princess Betsy

Princess Varvara

Countess Ivanova

1

An Unhappy Marriage

Happy families are all the same, but unhappy families are unhappy in different ways.

Stiva Oblonsky had just woken up in his house in Moscow. It was eight o'clock and he had spent the night on the couch in his study. He sat up and looked around the room.

'Why am I here?' he asked himself. And then he remembered. The Oblonsky family was a very unhappy one at the moment and it was all his fault. Stiva sighed.

'Dolly will never forgive me, this time!' he said out loud. 'Why was I so careless? Why did I let her find out? That little French governess was such a pretty girl! But there are lots of pretty girls in Moscow that my wife knows nothing about. This time, she knows everything and how very angry she is!'

And indeed, Stiva's poor, unhappy wife Dolly, had stayed in her room for three days. She was refusing to speak to him and their five children were running wild around the house and doing what they liked.

The servants had guessed everything, of course, and some of them had already left. Others were not doing any work at all. Everything was untidy and meals were not being served on time.

Stiva stood up and sighed again. 'Well, it's not all my fault,' he said to himself. 'I am still only thirty-four and I enjoy having a good time. I can't resist a pretty woman, but not many young men can. Dolly is looking old these days, but I still love her. I know it's hard work looking after the house and five children – but she's a married woman and that's her job. I'd better go and speak to her now and tell her how sorry I am. Perhaps I can calm her down and get her to understand.'

In her bedroom, Dolly was crying and trying to pack. She looked up angrily as Stiva walked in with his usual happy smile.

'I've sent my sister Anna a telegram. She will arrive here tomorrow,' Stiva said. 'I would like you to talk to her.'

Dolly's pale, thin face was covered with tears.

'I can't welcome your sister to my home when I look like this,' she replied quickly. 'Anyway, I probably won't be here. I am thinking of taking the children to my mother's.'

'I know how you feel, but please do forgive me, Dolly,' her husband said. 'We've been married for nine years and we have been happy, haven't we? Please don't leave me now. How could I live without you and the children? I only . . .'

'You only?' Dolly repeated angrily. 'You *only* had an affair with your children's governess! You only let the servants know everything! I hate you! Get out of this room and out of this house. Go and live with your mistress! You can laugh with her about me. Just go away. I never want to see you again.'

At that moment, a child began to cry in the room next door. Dolly listened and her angry expression suddenly softened.

'Well, at least she loves her child – my child,' Stiva thought to himself. 'My dear Dolly, just let me . . .' he began.

'I'm busy. Leave me alone,' Dolly replied quickly. 'If you follow me, I shall tell the servants to send you away. Now I must go and look after the child.'

As she went out of the room, she banged the door behind her. Her husband sighed.

'I'll try to talk to her later,' he said to himself. 'I can't bear all this shouting. I'll leave her alone for a time. Anna will be here soon. She will know what to say and I think Dolly will listen to her. I suppose I'd better go to the office now.'

Dolly Oblonskaya heard the front door bang shut behind her husband and the sound of his carriage driving away. Then she returned to her bedroom. She sat down and began to cry. As she cried, she turned her rings round and round on her thin fingers.

'He has gone! But has he gone to her?' she asked herself. 'Oh, how I loved him! How I loved him! Even now, I love him more than ever, but we are strangers in our own house.'

But her thoughts were interrupted as a servant came into the room and asked about the children's food. Dolly stopped crying and stood up.

'I shall see about it at once,' she told the servant.

Stiva Oblonsky was busy in his office all day. He did not work hard, but he always had something to do and someone to talk to. He was a popular man and his life had always been easy. He was good-looking and cheerful, and had many friends with whom he enjoyed talking and eating good, expensive food. Stiva enjoyed spending money – mostly on himself – and he never had enough of it.

One of his oldest friends called at his office that afternoon.

'Why, it's you, Levin, at last,' Oblonsky cried when he saw the tall bearded figure of Constantine Levin. 'What are you doing in Moscow? I thought you were busy in the country, looking after your peasants and working on your committees.'

'The country must carry on without me for a time and the committees bore me,' Levin replied. 'I have come to Moscow for a special reason. How are the Shcherbatskys?'

'Don't you mean "How is *Kitty* Shcherbatskaya?"' Oblonsky replied with a laugh.

'Tell me the truth. You're here to propose to Kitty, aren't you? Dolly will be delighted. Kitty's a pretty little girl, isn't she?'

Levin blushed and smiled, but he did not reply.

'Well, as Kitty is my sister-in-law, I ought to help you,' Oblonsky went on. 'The Shcherbatsky family ice-skates in the park from four to five every afternoon. Go and meet Kitty there. I can't ask you to dinner, because Dolly is not well. But I'll take you out for a meal tonight. Good luck with pretty little Kitty!'

Levin had known the Shcherbatsky family for many years and had been in love with Kitty Shcherbatskaya, their younger daughter, for a long time. But Levin had always believed that he was too dull and unattractive for her.

'I am just a countryman,' he had said to himself. 'I work hard and my land is good and well-farmed. I have money, but I have no real position in society and what would Kitty do in the country? She is only eighteen and she enjoys living in the city. She would find the country too dull – and me too.'

But after several months had gone by, Levin realised that his feelings for Kitty remained very strong. It was then that he decided he had to return to Moscow to tell her how he felt. He needed to know for sure whether she would marry him or not.

'I love her and I must tell her so,' Levin thought as he left Stiva's office. 'I have come to Moscow to propose to Kitty Shcherbatskaya and that is what I am going to do! I shall meet her in the park. At least I have not forgotten how to ice-skate!'

2
Rivals

Levin was a tall, heavy man, but he was a very fine skater. As soon as he reached the skating rink in the park, he hired some skates. In a very short time, he was moving elegantly around on the ice. As he skated, he looked around for Kitty Shcherbatskaya and his heart began to beat fast.

And then he saw her. To Levin, Kitty was surrounded by a beautiful light. She made everything around her seem brighter.

'Can I really go up to her and ask her to skate with me?' Levin said to himself. Then, to his joy, Kitty saw him and began skating towards him. She was even more lovely than he remembered. She was very slim and with her fair hair and sweet smile, she looked like a pretty child.

Kitty was not skating very steadily. Without thinking, Levin moved forward and took her hand.

'Thank you,' she said with a smile. 'I don't skate very well. I need more practice. But I remember what a good skater you are.'

'I wanted to be the best,' Levin said. 'I wanted to be perfect.'

'I think that you do everything perfectly,' Kitty said. 'Will you skate with me?'

'Yes!' Levin thought to himself, as they skated off together, side by side. 'This is happiness!' They went faster and faster. The faster they went, the more tightly Kitty held Levin's hand.

'I skate better with you. You give me confidence,' Kitty said.

'And when I am with you, I have more confidence too,' Levin replied boldly.

'Are you here for long?' Kitty asked.

Levin took a deep breath. Then he said, 'I don't know. That depends on you.'

Kitty did not seem to hear his words, or perhaps she did not wish to hear them. She let go of his hand and skated away towards her mother.

'Oh, God, why did I say that?' Levin said to himself. 'Now I have ruined everything!'

He skated slowly towards the Shcherbatskys and to his joy, saw that Kitty and her mother were smiling. Levin was invited to the Shcherbatskys' home that evening.

Levin left the ice-rink with Oblonsky, who took him out to dinner as he had earlier promised to do.

Both men wanted to talk about their love life. Stiva Oblonsky was anxious to talk about his problems with Dolly. Levin only wanted to talk about his hope of a future with Kitty.

'Dolly thinks that you will marry her sister,' Oblonsky told his friend. 'She is usually right about these things. But I have to tell you that you have a rival – Count Vronsky.'

Levin frowned.

'I don't know him,' he said. 'Does he live in Moscow?'

'Vronsky is a rich young man from Petersburg,' Stiva replied. 'He is a soldier and very good-looking. He's intelligent and well-educated too. He would be very suitable for Kitty, In fact, he started seeing her just after you left Moscow. He really seems to love Kitty and her mother approves of him, I hear.'

'I wish now that I had stayed in the country,' Levin said. 'What chance have I got with any woman, especially a beautiful young girl like Kitty? I should forget about women altogether.'

Oblonsky laughed.

Kitty did not seem to hear his words, or perhaps she did not wish to hear them.

Nearly all the young men who danced with Kitty that winter were in love with her. But Levin and Vronsky were her most serious suitors, or so everyone thought. Kitty's father was in favour of Levin, but her mother thought that Vronsky would be perfect for her pretty daughter. He was very rich, very handsome and had a great future as a soldier before him. So when Levin returned to Moscow, Kitty's mother was worried.

'Constantine Levin's had his chance,' she thought. 'If he proposes to Kitty now, she won't know what to say to him. I'm sure it's Vronsky that she loves!'

The truth was that Kitty was not sure at all. She wanted to be in love, but she did not know with whom.

'Constantine Levin is kind, but he is not very good-looking,' Kitty thought to herself. 'He is awkward too and does not enjoy society, as I do. He is always very serious and I have often found his ideas difficult to understand. However, Alexei Vronsky is charming and he always makes me feel pretty and happy. But Vronsky's family is an important one in Petersburg society and everyone likes him. Does he really want to marry me?'

Levin had no idea what Kitty was thinking. He went straight to the Shcherbatskys' house. When he came into the sitting-room, Kitty was there by herself.

'I am too early,' he said to her. 'But I wanted to find you alone. I have come to Moscow for one reason – to see you!'

'No, no,' he said. 'We men can't live without women. Our lives are pointless without them. My problem is that I can love more than one woman at a time. Dolly cannot understand that.'

'Neither can I,' Levin said seriously. 'Married men and women should be faithful to one another. I shall speak to Kitty tonight. Pay for the meal, Stiva. I'm going to the Shcherbatskys'.'

Levin took a deep breath, then went on quickly. 'I came to say, that is . . . I want you to be my wife, my dearest Kitty!'

Then he stopped speaking and looked at Kitty. She was breathing very fast. At first, Levin's proposal had excited her, but then she had thought of Vronsky.

'No, that cannot be – forgive me,' she said quickly.

'It is as I thought,' Levin said sadly. He turned to leave the room, but at that moment, Kitty's mother came in. She realised what had happened at once.

'Good, she has refused him,' she thought to herself, but she smiled at Levin and spoke to him politely.

A few minutes later, an officer came into the room. Levin watched Kitty's eyes shine as she saw the handsome young man.

'That must be Vronsky, my rival,' he thought to himself. 'There is no hope for me.'

Vronsky was a broad-shouldered young man of medium height. His dark hair was cut short and his face had a happy, confident expression.

'Constantine Levin, I think I met you earlier this winter,' Vronsky said with a smile, as he held out his hand. 'I understand that you live in the country. I would find that rather dull.'

'It's not dull at all,' Levin answered quickly. 'There is always so much to do. I shall be leaving Moscow in a day or two. There is nothing to keep me here.'

'Then you will miss the ball next week,' Vronsky said. 'That will be a pity.'

When Kitty's mother told her husband about what had happened between Levin and Kitty, he became very angry.

'You and Kitty may agree that Vronsky is handsome and charming, but he has no intention of marrying anyone,' her husband cried. 'Kitty will be as unhappy as poor Dolly. Levin is a thousand times better than Vronsky but you women all love a handsome face. You will never learn. I despair of you all!'

'Nonsense!' his wife cried. 'Vronsky's mother is coming to Moscow tomorrow – he is only waiting for her to arrive. Then he will propose to Kitty, I know he will.'

But Kitty's father was right. Vronsky was delighted by Kitty's beauty and innocence, but he had no intention of marrying her, or anyone else. Vronsky had had many affairs with actresses and dancers in Petersburg, but they had never been serious.

Levin returned to his home in the country the next day. He was deeply unhappy and he felt that his visit to Moscow had been a wasted one. Kitty Shcherbatskaya was even more beautiful than he had remembered.

'She is very young, but she is a pure, good woman,' Levin thought as he travelled home. 'I cannot live alone – what is the point of that? I work hard, but why do I do it? I need a wife. I need a family to complete my life. I love Kitty – she is the only woman I will ever love and now I have lost her.'

In a few days, Levin was soon busy with the work on his farm. He tried hard to forget his rejection29 by Kitty Shchbatskaya, but the pain in his heart would not go away.

3

At the Station

At eleven o'clock the next morning, Vronsky and Oblonsky met by chance at the railway station. They shook hands.

'Hallo, Count, who are you meeting?' Oblonsky cried.

'My mother,' Vronsky replied. 'She is travelling here from Petersburg. What about you?'

'I'm meeting a very pretty girl – my sister Anna,' Oblonsky said. 'She's Karenin's wife. You must know Karenin as you live in Petersburg. He's an important man there.'

'Alexei Karenin? I think I may have met him,' Vronsky said. 'He's very clever I believe, though rather cold. We don't really have the same friends or interests,' he added with a smile.

'I believe you met Constantine Levin, yesterday,' Oblonsky went on. 'He's a good friend of mine.'

'Yes. But like most of you people who live in Moscow, he seemed angry about something,' replied Vronsky.

There was the sound of a train whistling in the distance. Then there was a rush of people towards the edge of the platform. Through the foggy, frosty air, the peasant workers could be seen slowly crossing the rails.

'You're wrong about Levin,' Oblonsky went on. 'He's very honest and he has a good heart. But he came to Moscow for a special reason.'

Vronsky looked hard at Oblonsky. 'Did Levin propose to your sister-in-law last night?' he asked.

'It's possible,' Oblonsky said. 'He has been in love with Kitty for a long time. She must have refused him, the silly girl.'

'I suppose so,' Vronsky said. 'It's often painful for us when we take women too seriously. But here comes the train.'

The platform began to shake as the train drew in. Vronsky was amused and delighted by the thought that Kitty had rejected Levin. 'That makes me the better man,' he thought.

extract taken from Anna Karenina by Leo Tolstoy

Answer key

1A Consuming passions

Leisure interests

1 2 take 3 keen 4 give, get 5 got
6 passion 7 obsessed 8 into 9 aficionado
10 crazy

Verb forms review

2 1 's 2 has 3 be 4 is 5 have 6 was
7 did 8 been

3 1 Was I? 2 Has she? 3 Does he? 4 Have you?
5 Had she? 6 Were they? 7 Did it? 8 Are you?

🔘 Dictation

4 🔘 **01**
1 I'd never really been interested in photography until my dad bought me a camera.
2 I've been collecting postcards as a hobby since I was about eight years old.
3 I can't understand people who get obsessive about their hobbies. Haven't they got anything better to do?
4 I really admire those people who have managed to make their hobby into a job.

1B Paintballing

Negatives & questions

1 1 Paintballing isn't / is not dangerous.
2 It doesn't / does not teach people to use firearms.
3 Paintballers don't / do not often have violent tendencies.
4 It hasn't / has not been used for military training purposes in a number of countries.
5 Players haven't / have not been killed in paintballing accidents.
6 Paintmarkers don't / do not look like real guns.
7 Paintballing wasn't / was not very popular ten years ago.
8 Paintballing didn't / did not start out as a game.

2 1 is 2 isn't 3 don't hear
4 did you get 5 Did you do 6 gave
7 didn't follow / wasn't following 8 was
9 Did you get 10 didn't know 11 didn't find
12 are you working

Saying *no*

3 1 I'm afraid not 2 Not to my knowledge
3 Are you kidding? 4 Not especially
5 Not exactly 6 I wish I could

Translation

4 Translate the text into your language. Check with your teacher.

1C Autograph hunters

Time adverbials

1 1 begin 2 while 3 first 4 end 5 afterwards
6 finally

2 1 to begin with, at first 2 in the end, finally
3 after a while, then, afterwards

Vocabulary from the lesson

3 1 c backstage 2 b exception 3 a shoulder
4 c premiere 5 b signature 6 c blank
7 b stock 8 c latter

4 1 b 2 f 3 e 4 d 5 a 6 c 7 g

Translation

5 Translate the text into your language. Check with your teacher.

1D Collectors

What clauses

1 1 c 2 f 3 b 4 a 5 d 6 e

2 1 What you don't understand *is* he's happy enough as he is.
2 What you need to do *is* find something to occupy your time.
3 What Bob wants *is* a bit of peace and quiet after a hard day at work.
4 What you could do *is* arrange for both of you to go out with friends.
5 What your friends can do *is* suggest some other activities outside the house.
6 What you really need to do *is* stop worrying!

3 1 What I was just telling Bob was that he should take up a hobby.
2 What he really needs is to get out of the house sometimes.
3 What I've suggested is he should give fishing a try.
4 What I mean is, it's very relaxing and it would get him out in the fresh air.
5 What Bob thinks is it would be boring.
6 What he'd prefer to do is stay at home and read a good book.
7 What he says is I'm obsessed with unnecessary hobbies.

Expressions with *thing*

4 1 another 2 about 3 past 4 in 5 for
6 good 7 those

🔘 Dictation

5 🔘 **02**
A: What've you bought them for? You've got hundreds of pairs already.
B: They were a bargain and you know I'm crazy about high heels.
A: What goes through your mind when you're in a shoe shop would keep a psychologist busy for years.
B: Oh come on, it's just one of those things. It's no worse than your obsession with movie memorabilia.

1 Reading

1 1 f The popularity of the game 2 b How to play
3 c World Championships 4 a How it started

5 e The meaning of the word   6 d Sudoku on TV

2 1 False   2 True   3 False   4 True   5 False
   6 False   7 True

3 1 e The puzzle was an overnight sensation and Sudoku had become a household word.
   2 f Unlike crosswords, anyone can do it.
   3 b However, she practises for two hours a day and is a regular visitor to the top Sudoku websites.
   4 d The magazine is now hoping that its new game, Kakuro, will prove to be equally popular.
   5 c Other names include 'Squared Away', 'Single Number' and 'Nine Numbers'.
   6 a According to the rules of the game, only games with one solution are permitted.

4 1 off   2 up   3 in   4 through   5 out   6 into
   7 up

Read & listen

6 03 Refer to Reading 1 *All you need to know about … Sudoku* on page 9.

2A Wildlife

Adjectives

1 1 inquisitive   2 cute   3 obedient   4 tame
   5 aggressive   6 ferocious   7 cold-blooded
   8 playful

2 1 aggressive   2 ferocious / aggressive
   3 cold-blooded   4 inquisitive   5 obedient   6 cute
   7 tame   8 playful

Present habits

3 1 are often growing   2 are often attacking
   3 will forever issue   4 will constantly ignore
   5 are often feeding   6 have come

Translation

4 Translate the text into your language. Check with your teacher.

2B Animal rights

Verb idioms

1 1 interrupting   2 make sense   3 misunderstood
   4 explaining   5 accept   6 saying 'no' to

2 1 add up   2 face   3 drawn the line
   4 missed the point   5 butted in   6 clear it up

Expressing opinions

3
A
1 wrong   2 ask   3 concerned   4 convinced
B
5 don't   6 think   7 honest   8 Personally

4 1 & c   2 & d   3 & a   4 & b

Dictation

5 04

To be honest, I can understand why people don't like them. I mean, they're not exactly docile, are they? But it's absurd to say they'd hurt anybody. A playful little bite on the nose, maybe, but they won't mean any harm. They always know when to draw the line.

2C Companions

Past habits

1 1 I remember that my grandmother used to have a beautiful garden.
   2 She would spend hours in her garden in summer, watering the plants and tending the flowers.
   3 She didn't use to like us playing near the flower beds.
   4 So she built a special playground where we would spend hours and hours every holiday.
   5 We used to love that playground and I was really sorry when she moved into a smaller house.
   6 She still had a garden, but it wasn't so big and on our weekly visits we would play inside the house instead.

2 3 had   5 grew   6 was   10 lived

Strong reactions

3 1 went   2 drives   3 go   4 about / on
   5 like   6 must

4 1 blows   2 up   3 lose   4 head   5 livid
   6 round   7 totally

Dictation

5 05

A: You shouldn't complain. It used to be far worse in his father's days.
B: Was he completely round the bend, too?
A: Totally insane. He used to have conversations with a turkey.
B: But I don't suppose the turkey would make as much mess as the ninety-eight cats?
A: No, but it would make a lot more noise.

2D Working animals

Be/Get used to

1 1 get   2 I'm   3 got   4 are
   5 is   6 get

2 1 get used to   2 used to   3 used to   4 are used to
   5 used to   6 get used to   7 used to   8 are used to
   9 are (not) used to

Collocations with *get*

3 1 I first got involved with voluntary work when I was at university.
   2 To start with, I didn't really get along with our new neighbours.
   3 Get on with it!
   4 Getting around by car in the centre of town can be quite stressful with all the traffic jams.
   5 I'll get in touch with you as soon as I hear any news.
   6 I've been doing loads of exercise but I still seem to be getting fat.

4 You think you have problems? I have problems! This morning I had a big breakfast and arrived at work a little late. I had an argument with the boss, and then was fired. When I came back home, I received a call from my wife, who said it was time we divorced ... So I contacted my lawyer, who told me he had an urgent appointment, but I had the impression he was lying. Just as I thought things had become as bad as they possibly could, I ...

5 *Students' own answers*

Translation

6 Translate the sentences into your language. Check with your teacher.

2 Reading

1 'compost' – all the other words are connected to birds

2 1, 2 stupid / foolish 3, 4 a stupid, foolish person

3 1 E Mallee fowl   2 E Mallee fowl   3 D Cuckoo
4 B Geese   5 F Great Indian hornbill
6 A Adele penguin

4 1 f   2 b   3 e   4 a   5 d   6 c

5 1 rolls   2 flick   3 regurgitating   4 resemble
5 burying   6 ignore   7 seals

Read & listen

7 **06** Refer to Reading 2 *Bird Brains* on page 15.

3A Fashion statements

Compound adjectives

1 1 aged   2 going   3 shaven   4 hand
5 out   6 off

2 anti-establishment   knee-length   middle-class
never-ending   old-fashioned   short-lived

3 1 anti-establishment   2 knee-length
3 never-ending   4 short-lived   5 old-fashioned
6 middle-class

Vocabulary from the lesson

4 1 velvet   2 wide-collared   3 Ethnic   4 flared
5 patterns   6 Ripped   7 provocative   8 safety pins
9 make-up

Translation

5 Translate the text into your language. Check with your teacher.

3B The right look

Expressions with *look*

1 1 got   2 best   3 through   4 exchanged
5 sophisticated   6 have   7 feminine

2 1 d that he wasn't happy.
2 a she never lost her looks.
3 f and decided I didn't like him.
4 b if he was going to cry.
5 e a complete idiot!
6 c what happened to Bill!

3 1 **look 2**, 2   2 **look 2**, 3
3 **look 2**, 1   4 **look 1**, 2
5 **look 1**, 2   6 **look 1**, 1

Defining and non-defining relative clauses

4 1 who / that   2 which   3 which / that
4 which / that   5 who / that   6 which / that

5 2   3   5

Dictation

6 **07**
1 Deciding what shoes to wear is probably the most important fashion decision you need to make.
2 The style, brand and condition of your shoes say much more about you than all the rest of your clothes put together.
3 If your shoes look old and scruffy, no matter how smart your clothes, you will look scruffy too.
4 On the other hand, if your shoes are expensive and stylish then people will think the same of you.

3C Mirror images

Participle clauses

1 1 that/which depicts a young woman
2 that were held to be universal
3 she is dressed or undressed
4 which are now considered unattractive
5 who are starving themselves to death
6 where they are either posing for photographers or starring in the Hollywood blockbusters of the time

2 1 living and working in modern cities
2 growing up in today's consumer society
3 paid to represent beauty products
4 claiming to cover serious news stories
5 seen by millions of cinema-goers all over the world
6 made available on the internet

Vocabulary from the lesson

3 1 susceptible   2 cloud   3 blemish   4 spotlight
5 set   6 eating

4 1 abnormal   2 incomprehensible   3 pimple
4 puberty   5 self-doubt   6 stunning

Dictation

5 **08**
We should have the choice to do whatever we want with our faces and bodies without being punished by an ideology that is using attitudes, economic pressure, and even legal judgments regarding women's appearance to undermine us psychologically and politically.

3D Model behaviour

Slang

1 1 nuts   2 dumb   3 beat   4 a drag   5 a grand
6 psyched up   7 an airhead   8 blow

2 1 beat   2 blow   3 psyched up   4 a drag
5 airhead   6 dumb   7 nuts   8 grand

Addition

3 6, 3, 5, 1, 4, 2

Translation

4 Translate the extract from a magazine index into your language. Check with your teacher.

3 Reading

2
1 d So, how did you get started?
2 b How long have you been doing it?
3 c Are all lookalikes professional actors?
4 e And what kind of work do you do most?
5 a Have you got any plans for a change of career?

3
1 c is a big fan of Marilyn Monroe
2 a at a fancy dress party
3 b be an actress
4 b one of the most requested lookalikes
5 b aren't sure if they want to open a lookalikes agency

4 1 get in touch   2 an audition   3 in character
4 wig   5 facial expressions / mannerisms
6 mannerisms / facial expressions   7 double up
8 competitive

🎧 Read & listen

5 🎧 **09** Refer to Reading 3 *How to be a celebrity lookalike* on page 21.

4A Living in fear

Word building

1 1 distressing   2 fearful / fearless
3 harmful / harmless   4 painful / painless
5 reasonable   6 relaxing   7 risky   8 successful

2 1 fearless   2 unreasonable   3 anxieties
4 cautious   5 painful   6 possibility

Explaining reasons

3 1 e James always tried to make sure that his office could contact him. Otherwise, he suffered from terrible anxiety.
2 a He bought an expensive mobile phone in order to be online all the time.
3 h It was important that people could contact him in case there was an emergency.
4 d He chose one with a solar battery so that he never ran out of power.
5 c It was a waterproof model so that he could take it in the shower.
6 g He carried it with him at all times in case it rang.
7 f He slept next to his phone. Otherwise, he was afraid of not hearing it.
8 b He put the volume on 'extra loud' in order to be sure of hearing it.

4 *Sample answers:*
1 He's wearing a mask. Otherwise, it would be dangerous.
2 He's wearing a mask in order to protect himself.
3 He's wearing a mask so that he doesn't breathe the virus.
4 He's wearing a mask in case there is something dangerous in the air.

🎧 Dictation

5 🎧 **10**
1 There's no harm in trying.
2 Why can't you be reasonable for once?
3 Put it down. Otherwise, you'll get hurt.
4 I'll say that again in case anyone didn't hear.
5 In order not to make this painful, I'll be quick.
6 I'll spell it out very carefully so that you can't get it wrong.

4B Gladiators

Present perfect and past simple

1 Rome is one of Europe's oldest cities but it ~~isn't always hasn't~~ always been the capital of Italy – since Rome ~~is only~~ has only been an official part of Italy since 1870. The city ~~changes~~ has changed a lot in recent years. It has the fastest-growing economy of any Italian city and its population of two and a half million includes many immigrants. Rome ~~always attracts~~ has always attracted people from outside the city, and, by tradition, a 'true' Roman family ~~lives~~ has lived there for more than seven generations.

2 1 Have you ever been   2 've just come   3 Was it
4 've been   5 went   6 met   7 've fallen
8 Was it   9 've been   10 got   11 Have you told
12 laughed   13 said   14 met

Vocabulary from the lesson

3 1 assertive   2 bossy   3 confident   4 domineering
5 reserved   6 self-assured   7 timid

Translation

4 Translate the text into your language. Check with your teacher.

4C The land of the brave

Word class

1 Nouns: abolition, disobedience, freedom, liberation, liberty, move, movement, rebellion, religion
Verbs: abolish, disobey, free, liberate, move
Adjectives: disobedient, free, rebellious, religious

2 **February 11th 1990** South Africa's first black president, Nelson Mandela, tastes liberty for the first time in 27 years.
May 6th 1862 Henry David Thoreau, American author of the essay 'Civil Disobedience', dies of tuberculosis.
May 12th 1916 James Connolly, leader of the failed rebellion against the British, is executed in a Dublin gaol.
October 15th 1969 Millions of Americans take part in demonstrations organized by the anti-war movement, calling for an end to the fighting in Vietnam.
November 1st 1998 The European Convention on Human Rights requires all members of the EU to abolish the death penalty.
December 10th 1948 The United Nations Universal Declaration of Human Rights declares that all people have freedom of thought, conscience and religion.

Vocabulary from the lesson

3 1 spark   2 regains   3 boycott   4 overturned
5 mass   6 backs   7 granted   8 racial

🎧 Dictation

4 🎧 **11**
Montgomery, Alabama, is not only famous for the bus boycott that shook the city in the 1950s. The state capital was also the first capital of the pro-slavery south during the Civil War. More than fifty percent of the popuation of over 200,000 are black. Martin Luther King, winner of the Nobel Peace Prize in 1964, was a church minister in Montgomery from 1954 to 1960. He was murdered in 1968.

4D Southern snakes

Present perfect simple & continuous

1 1 been being   6 been agreeing   8 been coming

2 1 have been reading / 've read
2 've saved / 've been saving
3 's been driving / 's driven
4 's had / 's been having
5 have been doing / have done

3 1 has been preparing   2 has done
3 has been following   4 has bought
5 has been looking   6 has spent
7 has studied / has been studying
8 has practised / has been practising   9 has left

Translation

4 Translate the text into your language. Check with
your teacher.

4 Reading

1 1 a   2 d   3 b   4 c

2 1 D   2 A   3 C   4 D   5 C   6 B   7 C   8 A
9 A

3 1 coming down, descent, landing
2 connecting, fitted to, linked to
3 device, flying machine, invention

4 *Students' own answers*

Read & listen

6 **12** Refer to Reading 4 *Flying lessons* on page 27.

5A Performance art

Narrative tenses

1 Staff at FBI Headquarters in Washington DC had never
given much thought to art. But, with the realization that
the country was ~~been~~ losing as much as $2 billion each
year, the FBI ~~did~~ set up the Art Crime Team in 2004.
Twelve special agents ~~were~~ joined the team after they
had ~~been~~ received special training in art crime. The
agents ~~had~~ began to track down a long list of missing
art works. By the end of their first year of operations,
they had ~~being~~ recovered items worth over $50 million.
These ~~were~~ included a self-portrait by Rembrandt which
~~did~~ had been stolen from the National Museum in
Stockholm.

2 1 was living   2 was   3 had had   4 were growing
5 was   6 had spent   7 had already died
8 was beginning   9 lived

3 artist   collection   dealer   exhibition   landscape
patron   sculpture   mural   figurative   still life
portrait   gallery   painter

4 1 artist   2 collection   3 sculpture   4 mural
5 portrait   6 gallery   7 still life

Dictation

5 **13**
In Stockholm earlier today, it was announced that three
thieves had walked into the National Museum and stolen
three masterpieces, including a self-portrait by Rembrandt.
A police spokesman said that the paintings had probably
left the country already. He said that they were working on
the theory that the paintings had been stolen to order.

5B Priceless!

-*ever* words

1 *Sample answers:*
1 he was   2 you do   3 happens / you do / you say
4 you do / you say   5 did that   6 you are

2 1 However   2 Whoever   3 whatever   4 wherever
5 Whenever   6 whatever   7 Wherever

Evaluating

3 1 masterpiece   2 fortune   3 priceless   4 valuable
5 rubbish   6 redeeming   7 worthless   8 worth

Translation

4 Translate the two dialogues in exercise 3 into your
language. Check with your teacher.

5C A good read

Past perfect continuous

1 1 Her husband had been seeing other women.
2 She had been sleeping at the time.
3 She had been standing in the sun for hours.
4 She had been thinking about it for ages.
5 She had been trying for four years.
6 The crowd had been growing for hours.
7 The children had been eating their dinner in front of
the TV.

2 1 c Mandy had to face the awful truth
2 d She heard absolutely nothing.
3 b It was no surprise that she fainted.
4 a Helen decided to take early retirement.
5 g She was delighted to learn that she was
finally pregnant.
6 e The atmosphere was electric.
7 f There were stains all over the sofa.

3 1 had only just turned   2 had been writing
3 had started   4 had been cycling   5 had become
6 had criticized   7 had been working   8 had won
9 had been protesting

Dictation

4 **14**
There's no question that *The God of Small Things* is a
masterpiece. Set in a town in southern India, it tells the
story of a woman and her family who have to return to the
family home after she gets divorced. The plot is revealed
from the children's point of view, with the narrative
switching between the present and the past.

5D Bookworm

Phrasal verbs 1

1 1 e so many original ideas.
2 d her reputation.
3 f the characters in her novels.
4 c her first attempt to write a novel.
5 a a charitable foundation.
6 b her children.

2 1 I don't know how she comes up with them.
2 It's not easy living up to it.
3 People really take to them.
4 The publishers turned it down.
5 With the money from her fifth book, she set it up.
6 She moved out of the city to bring them up.

Vocabulary from the lesson

3 1 c glance 2 a classic 3 b detention
4 a short 5 a inspired 6 b god-send
7 a grab

4 1 e a romantic novel 2 b a book review
3 c a news item 4 g competition rules
5 a a biography 6 d a personal letter
7 f an advertisement

Translation

5 Translate the text into your language. Check with your teacher.

5 Reading

2 1 C 2 E 3 A 4 B 5 D

3 1 And with my painting, I have to paint alone.
2 I prefer it when other people bring their own interpretations to my work.
3 I worked as an actor for ten years. But you have to make a living. One of the reasons, I guess, why I do different things.
4 You have to be your own salesman, your own agent.
5 What you want to express as a painter, isn't necessarily something that people out there want to buy.
6 Some of the Japanese designs are fantastic.
7 If I hadn't been a painter, I'd have been a performance artist.
8 My mother helped me learn to draw.

4 1 his mother
2 painting the skin
3 Central Saint Martin's College of Arts and Design in London
4 the tattoo on his ankle
5 being a plastic surgeon
6 the people in Montreal

🔊 Read & listen

5 🔊 **15** Refer to Reading 5 *Michel Soucy* on page 33.

6A At the polls

Real and unreal conditions

1 1 Anyone can become the president of the US provided they want to badly enough and they're ready to work hard to get what they want.
2 Don't enter politics unless you know exactly why you're doing it and what you want out of it.
3 He might have won the election if he hadn't lost his temper and insulted his opponent live on TV.

4 I would only enter politics so long as I could guarantee the privacy of my wife and children.
5 I'll give up my post as governor on condition that I can run for President.
6 He would never have been so successful if it hadn't been for his wife.
7 I would never, ever consider a life in politics, unless, of course, I was asked to.
8 If you want a career in politics you'll have to be prepared to give up everything else, friends, family and all your free time.

2 Sentences 1, 2, 5 & 8 are real conditions.
Sentences 3, 4, 6 & 7 are unreal conditions.

3 1 If you pick up a starving dog and make him prosperous, he <u>will</u> not bite you. This is the principal difference between a man and a dog. (Mark Twain)
2 If we couldn't laugh, <u>we'd</u> all go insane. (Jimmy Buffet)
3 There is a theory which states that if ever anybody <u>discovers</u> exactly what the Universe is for and why it is here, it will instantly disappear and be replaced by something even more bizarre and unexplicable. (Douglas Adams)
4 Americans will put up with anything provided it <u>doesn't</u> block traffic. (Dan Rather)
5 Nobody <u>will believe</u> in you unless you believe in yourself. (Liberace)
6 Oh, I don't blame Congress. If I <u>had</u> $600 billion at my disposal, I'd be irresponsible too. (Lichty and Wagner)

💿 Dictation

4 💿 **16**
1 If I hadn't seen it with my own eyes, I wouldn't have believed it.
2 I'll believe it when I see it.
3 He'll do anything you ask of him, provided you pay him enough money.
4 I would never, ever consider doing anything like that, unless you paid me.
5 If I'd known, I wouldn't even have spoken to him.

6B Women in politics

I wish/If only

1 1 c 2 b 3 d 4 e 5 f 6 a

2 1 'd known 2 were 3 hadn't done
4 wasn't / weren't raining 5 'd been

Elections

4 1 Members 2 turnout 3 polling 4 constituency
5 ballot 6 candidate 7 general

Vocabulary from the lesson

5 1 involved 2 set 3 run 4 step 5 voted
6 fight 7 represented 8 committed

Translation

6 Translate the poem into your language. Check with your teacher.

6C Politically incorrect

Embarrassment

1 7, 1, 3, 8, 2, 5, 6, 4

Should have

2 1 b 2 a 3 a 4 b 5 b 6 a 7 a 8 b

3 *Sample answers:*
The US shouldn't have fought a war against the Lakota.
The US forces shouldn't have broken the treaty.
Custer shouldn't have been made leader of a cavalry division.
Custer shouldn't have advanced faster than the rest of the army.
Custer shouldn't have ignored his orders.
He should have listened to the advice of his scouts.
He shouldn't have divided his men into three groups.

Dictation
4 **17**
I recognize that this government has made a serious mistake and that we should not have taken these steps without consulting the people. I realize that I, personally, should have been better informed earlier and I should certainly have been more honest in the last few months. I can only agree with those people who say that I should have resigned earlier. I was wrong and I apologize.

6D Politically correct

-isms
1 1 a anti-sexist   2 b idealist
3 b socialist   4 b pacifist   5 b realist

2 1 atheist   2 anarchist   3 fatalist   4 materialist
5 individualist   6 capitalist

Asking for & giving clarification
3 1 know   2 suggesting   3 follow   4 mean
5 basically   6 meant   7 point   8 words

Translation
4 Translate the text into your language. Check with your teacher.

6 Reading
1 cynical

2 A 2 BBC man Bell found not guilty
B 1 British MPs in cash for questions scandal
C 1 Al-Fayed celebrates victory over Hamilton
D 2 Hamilton loses count to Bell

3 1 B   2 D   3 A   4 C

4 1 A   2 C   3 A   4 A   5 A   6 C   7 B   8 B

5 1 overturned   2 found   3 accused   4 declare
5 clear   6 denied   7 faces   8 surfaced

Read & listen
6 **18** Refer to Reading 6 *Cash-for-questions* on page 38.

7A Green issues

The environment
1 1 warming   2 gases   3 fumes   4 wind   5 solar
6 change   7 food

Vocabulary from the lesson
2 car tyres   chronic illnesses   carrier bags
coastal areas   fire retardants   organic crops
printer ink   plant dyes

3 1 organic crops   2 coastal areas   3 chronic illnesses
4 carrier bags   5 plant dyes   6 car tyres
7 printer ink   8 fire retardants

Dictation
4 **19**
Change in the Earth's climate and its adverse effects are a common concern of humankind.
Human activities have been substantially increasing the atmospheric concentrations of greenhouse gases. These increases enhance the natural greenhouse effect, and this will result, on average, in an additional warming of the Earth's surface and atmosphere.

7B Green houses

Futures review
1 1 it's going to be   2 will rise   3 are meeting
4 will not decrease   5 they're going to have
6 I'll grab

2 1 are you going to fix   3 is coming   6 I have
8 I've got   10 I'm seeing   11 are you doing

Expressions with *make*
3 1 for   2 with   3 to   4 for   5 of   6 for   7 of
8 to

Translation
4 Translate the text into your language. Check with your teacher.

7C Lifestyle changes

Future perfect & future continuous
1 1 Heather is training to become a life coach. As soon as she's qualified, she'll <u>be</u> looking for work.
2 But before she earns anything, she'll <u>have</u> spent over $1000 on her training.
3 She'll <u>be</u> having her next class at 3 o'clock on Tuesday afternoon.
4 After that, she'll <u>have</u> done nearly two-thirds of the course.
5 She'll <u>be</u> taking her final exam in December.
6 If she passes that, she'll <u>be</u> starting her 'experience programme' immediately afterwards.
7 She hopes she will <u>have</u> completed all her training by next summer.

2 *Sample answers:*
1 She'll be working on her portfolio this week, she'll be attending a roleplay workshop at 2.30 pm on Tuesday, she'll be having dinner with her classmates on Saturday evening.
2 She'll have finished her portfolio by Thursday evening, she'll have done two coaching observations by the end of the week, she'll have started work on her fifth assignment before next week.

Vocabulary from the lesson
3 1 c   2 b   3 b   4 a   5 b   6 c   7 a   8 b

Dictation
4 **20**
A: By this time next year, I'll be making millions.
B: You mean you'll be looking for a job.
A: No, I'll have set up my own company.
B: I hope you won't be asking me to help you out.
A: Only once. You'll be lending me the money to start things off.
B: I certainly won't be doing anything of the sort.
A: Yes, you will. And we'll both be laughing all the way to the bank

7D Trends

Giving examples

1 6, 7, 1, 4, 5, 2, 3

2 If you want to find out about the future, there are many people, ~~among other things~~, who can help you. You can turn, *for example*, to the horoscope pages of ~~such as~~ the newspaper where you can find out about your love life, ~~in particular~~. For more serious information, you can dip into the writing of well-known prophets *such as* Nostradamus or use magical books *like* the I Ching, *to name but a few*. But if you're really serious ~~for instance~~ about the future, you can take a course, ~~in particular~~, in Futures Studies. At the University of Budapest, *for instance*, you can study topics *like* 'Change and Future' or 'Space and Time in Futures Studies', *to name but two*.

Nouns & prepositions

3 1 The developing world's demand   2 The British taste
3 Rapid advances   4 A growing interest
5 An increase   6 Annual consumption
7 A shortage

Translation

4 Translate the quotations into your language. Check with your teacher.

7 Reading

1 1 d   2 b   3 c   4 a   5 e

2 1 a gossip and celebrities magazine
2 *Students' own answers*

3 b   c   d   e   f   i

4 1 Because the text tells us that 'it seems that many of the city's 20 million inhabitants are out shopping'.
2 Because she says she 'prefers to introduce herself simply as Helen Taylor'.
3 Because it was attended by a number of celebrities.
4 Because she talks about her experiences of acupuncture and osteopathy, and her bad back.
5 Because she has just signed her seventh contract to work for Armani and says she has a lot of fun.

5 1 'browsing at the stalls'
2 'it would be disingenuous to claim that it is not quite useful at times'
3 'roving ambassador'
4 'voracious appetite'
5 'I will always back the brand because I love his clothes.'

6 *Students' own answers*

🔊 Read & listen

7 🔊 **21** Refer to Reading 7 *Lady Helen Taylor* on page 45.

8A Cold comfort

Symptoms

1 1 c   2 e   3 b   4 f   5 d   6 a

2 1 stiff muscles   2 hacking cough   3 upset stomach
4 runny nose   5 high temperature
6 throbbing headache

3 A: 2, 3, 1
B: 2, 3, 1
C: 3, 1, 4, 2

Vocabulary from the lesson

4 1 's off   2 sounded   3 gone off   4 lose   5 take
6 come across

Translation

5 Translate the jokes into your language. Check with your teacher.

8B Bill of health

Health idioms

1 1 She was feeling a bit under the weather.
2 I think I am coming down with something.
3 There's definitely a bug going round.
4 My back was killing me.
5 He was given a clean bill of health.
6 I thought I was at death's door yesterday.

2 a 5   b 6   c 4   d 1   e 3   f 2

Modals of speculation

3 1 Anything ~~must~~ could/might have happened to her.
2 She ~~can~~ could/must have got lost.
3 She ~~mustn't~~ must have forgotten it at home.
4 That must ~~have been~~ be what she's doing.

4 1 can't have   2 mustn't have   3 might have been
4 couldn't have   5 can't   6 must   7 might have
8 must have been

5 *Students' own answers*

💿 Dictation

6 💿 **22**
1 She mightn't be telling the whole truth.
2 They couldn't have known we'd be here.
3 It can't have been anything to do with him.
4 I can only guess what it must have been like.
5 It may have been her and then again it might not.
6 Some of you might have missed what I was saying earlier.
7 You must have worked out some of the answers by now.

8C Alternative therapies

Modals (permission, obligation & prohibition)

1 1 weren't allowed to   2 had to   3 were allowed to
4 had to   5 can   6 have to   7 don't have to
8 mustn't   9 have to

2 1 have   2 had   3 allowed   4 were   5 don't
6 can   7 aren't   8 must

Vocabulary from the lesson

3 1 low morale   2 growing number   3 full spectrum
4 natural light   5 colour scheme
6 work-related illness   7 ergonomic keyboard

💿 Dictation

4 💿 **23**
1 Acupuncture has its roots in traditional Chinese medicine.
2 It involves inserting long, thin needles in the body at very specific points.
3 It is used to treat a wide variety of illnesses and medical conditions.
4 It is particularly popular in the treatment of chronic back pain.
5 It has even been tried with school pupils suffering from stress.

8D Back pain

Changing the subject
1 1 reminds   2 think   3 Talking   4 for   5 way
  6 saying

Phrasal verbs with objects
2 1 look after   2 get back to   3 putting it off
  4 drop off   5 call in   6 put up with
  7 talked us through the treatment   8 sort itself out

3 1 ~~get me back to~~ / get back to me
  2 ~~put it up with~~ / put up with it
  4 ~~give up it~~ / give it up
  5 ~~told off him~~ / told him off

Translation
4 Translate the dialogue into your language. Check with
your teacher.

8 Reading

1 Students' own answers

2 1, 4, 2, 3

3 5, 1, 6, 4, 2, 3

4 1 b   2 a   3 b   4 b   5 a   6 a   7 b

5 *Students' own answers*

🔊 Read & listen
6 🔊 **24** Refer to Reading 8 *The Unicorn in the Garden*
on page 51.

9A Celebrity heroes

Adjective order
1 1 stylish Italian leather dancing shoes
  2 4 exceptional-value original 1960s plastic dining
    chairs.
  3 amazing, life-size, full-colour poster of Natalie
    Portman
  4 unwanted pair of long, grey boxer shorts
  5 large, black, pointed wizard's hat
  6 beautiful miniature Venetian glass rose
  7 enormous, blue/yellow European flag
  8 brand new super-slim Japanese digital camera

2 1 a huge, black, satin tie
  2 a smelly, round, French cheese
  3 an old, grey, woollen jumper
  4 a long, square, wooden stick

Vocabulary from the lesson
3 1 e   2 c   3 d   4 f   5 g   6 a   7 b

4 1 with   2 of   3 on   4 of   5 into   6 to
  7 for   8 of   9 for   10 of   11 as

🔊 Dictation
5 🔊 **25**
Actor George Clooney has hit back at websites that
encourage members of the public to post sightings of
celebrities. These celebrity-watching sites are becoming
increasingly popular around the world and, according to
the Hollywood star, are a threat to the private lives and
safety of people in the public eye.

9B Local hero

Adjectives with prepositions
1 1 involved   2 devoted   3 intent   4 restricted
  5 connected   6 aware   7 sympathetic   8 familiar

2 1 of   2 to   3 in   4 to   5 from   6 on   7 for

Vocabulary from the lesson
3 1 triumphing   2 inconvenience   3 reveal
  4 citizenship   5 sighting   6 update   7 check out
  8 psychologist

Translation
4 Translate the text into your language. Check with
your teacher.

9C Villains

Adverbs & modifying adjectives
1 1 old / ancient   2 bad / awful   3 big / enormous
  4 hot / boiling   5 good / brilliant   6 cold / freezing
  7 important / crucial   8 happy / delighted
  9 difficult / impossible   10 tired / exhausted
  11 interested / fascinated

2 1 pretty / absolutely   2 really / exhausted
  3 a bit / quite   4 absolutely / slightly
  5 very / different   6 absolutely / totally

Crimes
3 1 mugging   2 armed robbery   3 smuggling
  4 vandalism   5 kidnapping   6 hijacking

🔊 Dictation
4 🔊 **26**
The number one, all-time screen villain who must be
on everybody's list is Hannibal Lecter. His cold-blooded
intelligence and total lack of respect for human life make
him a truly terrifying figure. And it is the relationship
between him and a young FBI agent that makes *The Silence
of the Lambs* one of the best horror movies ever made.

9D Hate list

Compound nouns (jobs)
1 1 jockey   2 agent   3 fighter   4 courier
  5 worker   6 inspector   7 rep   8 warden

2 1 park warden   2 student rep   3 disc jockey
  4 travel agent   5 health inspector   6 jet fighter
  7 drug courier   8 rescue worker

Contrast
3 1, 5, 6, 2, 4, 3

Vocabulary from the lesson
4 1 dashing   2 dazzling   3 slimy   4 bigoted
  5 vindictive   6 obnoxious   7 arrogant

Translation
5 Translate the sentences into your language. Check with
your teacher.

9 Reading

1 1 c 2 b 3 a 4 a 5 b 6 c 7 b

2 3 POW! Batman's universal appeal

3 a 4 b 2 c 1 d 5 e 3

4 a 5 b 1 c 3 d 3 e 1 f 4 g 4 h 2

5 1 peopled with 2 get their hands on
3 is plagued by 4 flock to 5 took to the streets
6 track down

6 *Students' own answers*

🔘 Read & listen

7 🔘 **27** Refer to Reading 9 *Batman* on page 57.

10A Good deeds

Reflexive verbs

1 1 You should consider yourself
2 Ask yourself
3 adapt yourself to
4 expressed yourself
5 content yourself
6 distinguish yourself

2 It is natural that parents endanger <u>themselves</u> in order to protect their young, both in the human and animal world. But this decision to sacrifice <u>themselves</u> for their children is not always the best choice. How will the children survive without their parents if they are too young to look after <u>themselves</u>? Parents need to remind <u>themselves</u> that they need to look after their own safety first, so that they are then in a better position to look after that of their children. This is also true in day-to-day life. Parents who dedicate <u>themselves</u> not only to their children, but also to their other interests and passions, make better parents. They should not consider <u>themselves</u> to be the slaves of their children, but rather pride <u>themselves</u> on being happy, satisfied individuals who share their love of life with their family.

Vocabulary from the lesson

3 1 from 2 to 3 for 4 to 5 against 6 from

4 1 benefit from 2 attach great importance to
3 sets us apart from 4 gave evidence against
5 sacrifice yourself 6 provide an answer to

Translation

5 Translate the proverbs into your language. Check with your teacher.

10B Giving

Reporting

1 1 if he wanted her to keep the jacket for him
2 he'd come back for it later that afternoon
3 they were giving it to charity
4 whether they'd be coming back the next day
5 he might be going away for a couple of days
6 when he thought he'd be getting back
7 he'd finished with it and didn't want it anymore

2 1 'Would you like me to keep the jacket for you?'
2 'I'll come back for it later this afternoon.'
3 'We're giving it to charity.'
4 'Will you be coming back tomorrow?'
5 'I might be going away for a couple of days.'
6 'When do you think you'll be getting back?'
7 'I've finished with it and I don't want it anymore.'

3 I asked him where ~~was his new jacket~~ *his new jacket was* and why ~~wasn't he~~ *he wasn't* wearing it. He said it had been stolen from his office. I asked him why ~~hadn't he~~ *he hadn't* told me and he said he ~~doesn't want to~~ *didn't want to / hadn't wanted to* upset me. When I told him I ~~had known~~ *knew* the truth, he said ~~was he~~ *he was* really sorry, he hadn't liked the jacket from the start, but he didn't know how to tell me.

4 1 they had found his jacket
2 if he knew about the money in the pocket
3 he was going to use it to pay a builder
4 her if she had the money with her
5 how much money he had left in the pocket
6 there should have been about two thousand pounds in twenty pound notes
7 why he had thrown the jacket away
8 he hadn't thrown it away; it was his ex-girlfriend who had thrown it away

Collocations with *give*

5 1 priority 2 consideration 3 problems 4 speech
5 permission 6 lecture 7 warning
8 piece of my mind

🔘 Dictation

6 🔘 **28**
Can you spare a coin or two, madam? I'm collecting for the poor and the homeless. You may have heard that the hostel for the homeless is going to close down next week, and I was wondering if you might like to give something for people less fortunate than ourselves?

10C Aid worker

Job responsibilities

1 1 promote 2 liaise 3 oversee 4 participate
5 coordinate 6 track 7 seek out 8 facilitate

2 1 participate 2 liaise 3 oversee 4 seek out
5 facilitate 6 promote 7 coordinate 8 track

Reporting verbs & patterns

3 1 They refused to have anything to do with the project.
2 He mentioned visiting our site in the North.
3 She admitted not knowing much about recent developments.
4 They invited us to come and see their new offices.
5 He promised to pass on the information as quickly as possible.
6 They denied having any connection whatsoever with the local authorities.
7 She encouraged me to try again.
8 They warned us not to travel through the mountains after dark.

4 After lengthy talks with our delegates, the local education authority has agreed ~~opening~~ *to open* four new schools in the area. We have managed to persuade them ~~putting~~ *to put* forward 50% of the funding and we have suggested ~~to spend~~ *spending* this money on the school buildings. In return the education authorities have asked us ~~supplying~~ *to supply* the teaching staff and materials.

Dictation

5 🔘 **29**

Working on grassroots development projects requires a great deal of patience and cultural sensitivity. You need to be able to assess the situation from various different points of view and encourage others to do the same. Above all, you must remember that your task is not to dictate changes, but to facilitate growth and development.

10D A good job

Job interviews

1 a to   b in   c for   d with   e as   f to   g at
   h in   i to   j on

2 a 2   b 3   c 5   d 4   e 1

Vocabulary from the lesson

3 1 meet   2 attending   3 giving   4 set   5 write
   6 develop

Translation

4 Translate the text into your language. Check with your teacher.

10 Reading

1 3

2 A Volunteer for Oxfam
   B Donate Now
   C Events supporting Oxfam
   D Recycle for Oxfam
   E Support us as you spend

3 f   h   i   j

4 *Sample answers:*
   1 a shop
   2 First edition: a copy of a book or other publication in its original, first printed form. Rare: of which there are very few copies available to buy.
   3 help themselves in overcoming poverty
   4 for the whole length of the trek, from beginning to end
   5 you've started a new phase in your life
   6 every mobile phone which is given to Oxfam in good working order

🔘 Read & listen

5 🔘 **30** Refer to Reading 10 *Oxfam* on page 62.

11A Globe-trotting

Geographical features

1 1 peninsula   2 ocean   3 canal   4 cape   5 falls
   6 bay   7 desert   8 strait

2 1 desert   2 falls   3 strait   4 bay   5 canal
   6 ocean

The & geographical names

3 The Straits of Magellan are named after the Portuguese explorer who first sailed through this narrow passage connecting the Atlantic and the Pacific. The Straits lead from the border between ~~the~~ Chile and ~~the~~ Argentina in the East, past the town of ~~the~~ Punta Arenas to the islands of the Queen Adelaide Archipelago in the West. It was the only safe route between the two oceans until 1914 when the Panama Canal was opened, enabling ships to sail right through ~~the~~ Central America. It was a popular route with prospectors trying to reach the coast of ~~the~~ California in the 1849 Gold Rush.

4 1 –   2 the   3 the   4 the   5 –   6 the   7 the

🔘 Dictation

5 🌐 **31**
1 The first people discovered America more than 10,000 years ago.
2 They came from the east, crossing the ice from Siberia to Alaska.
3 They discovered a land which was very similar to Siberia but with no people living there.
4 More people followed and they advanced down the west coast of the continent.
5 Eventually they occupied the whole of North and South America.

11B South is up

Binomials

1 1 short and sweet   2 –   3 bits and pieces
   4 black and white   5 –   6 forgive and forget

2 1 Tried / tested   2 Pick / choose   3 To / fro
   4 flesh / blood   5 here / now

Vague language

3 It's ~~kind of~~ difficult to say exactly what it is to be Australian. People talk about national identity ~~and stuff like that~~, but it's really much more personal. It's ~~stuff like~~ the things you do every day, your family, your friends ~~and so on~~ and the things you do together. The way we live our lives ~~sort of~~ defines who we are, and I suppose there is a lifestyle which could be called ~~more or less~~ typically Australian. It's a simple lifestyle, an outdoor lifestyle. It doesn't mean we're all sports mad, surfing or kayaking ~~or something~~ all day long, but it does mean that we tend to spend a lot of time outside, ~~you know~~, in our gardens, on the beach, taking it easy.

4 I've loved maps since I was a kid. I suppose they kind _of_ remind me of my dad. He had a huge one in his study. It covered the whole wall. It must have been like 5 metres long _or_ something. We used to spend hours just, you _know_, looking at the map and planning imaginary journeys and stuff _like_ that. We used to stick flags in it to show where we'd been on holiday and so _on_. And since I left home I've always, more _or_ less, had a map in my room. And my bookshelves are packed with them, road maps, street maps, atlases, globes and _so_ on. Some people say I'm obsessed and I guess they're sort _of_ right.

Translation

5 Translate the text into your language. Check with your teacher.

11C Positive psychology

Articles

1 1 the 2 Ø 3 a 4 the 5 the 6 the 7 the
8 the 9 a 10 the 11 Ø 12 a 13 Ø
14 Ø 15 Ø 16 Ø 17 the 18 the

2 Researchers believe that happiness, or '~~a~~ life satisfaction' occurs most frequently when people lose themselves in ~~the~~ daily activities. The term used to describe this is 'flow'. ~~A~~ people in flow may be doing something very simple, sewing a button on a shirt or cooking a meal. They may be involved in ~~a~~ work, playing a musical instrument, taking part in ~~the~~ sport or losing themselves in a good book. The result is always the same.

The important thing is to identify the activities in your ~~a~~ day-to-day life that absorb you most and to build your life around these things. That, it seems, is the secret of ~~the~~ true happiness.

Vocabulary from the lesson

3 1 Very often other people's perceptions of us are much more important than our bank balance.
2 There is no simple, straightforward correlation between happiness and money.
3 It is crucial to take a number of different factors into account.
4 It is also important to remember that we are looking at overall happiness and not single euphoric moments.
5 But having measured happiness levels we still need to tackle the basic problem of finding ways of making people happier.
6 The most affluent people in society are not necessarily the happiest.

Translation

4 Translate the text into your language. Check with your teacher.

11D Perfect locations

Describing landscape

1 1 estuary 2 hills 3 valleys 4 gorge 5 peaks
6 cliffs

So & such

2 1 such 2 so 3 so 4 so 5 so 6 such

3 1 It's been such a long time since I've seen a really good film.
2 The scenery was so incredibly beautiful that it was almost a distraction from the film.
3 It is such a simple story.
4 But the acting is so good that it really brings the story alive.
5 The closing scene was so sad, it made me cry.
6 It's such an excellent movie and I highly recommend it.

🔘 Dictation

4 🔘 **32**
A: Did you go out last night?
B: No, I was so tired, I stayed at home. I watched *Lord Of the Rings* on DVD instead.
A: It's such a great movie, isn't it?
B: Yeah, and the scenery is absolutely stunning.
A: So spectacular it makes you want to catch the next plane to New Zealand!
B: Yeah, possibly.

11 Reading

1

PARA	1	2	3	4	5	6
		B	D	C	A	

2 a 2 b 6 c 3 d 1 e 3 f 2 g 5 h 4

3 1 a 2 b 3 a 4 a 5 b 6 b 7 b

4 2, 4 and 6

5 *Students' own answers*

🔘 Read & listen

6 🔘 **33** Refer to Reading 11 *Making Slough Happy* on page 69.

12A Loot

Passives review

1 1 was reputedly worn 2 was auctioned 3 was
4 had ever been paid 5 consists 6 is held
7 was once owned 8 was bought

2 1 have been made 2 was first published
3 has been adapted 4 were written
5 were then read 6 has been translated
7 was paid 8 were never used (have never been used – if you consider that pirates are also a modern day phenomenon)

Vocabulary from the lesson

3 1 raid 2 track down 3 make off with
4 carry out 5 head for 6 threaten

🔘 Dictation

4 🔘 **34**
1 A cruise liner has been attacked by pirates off the Eastern coast of Africa.
2 It is the first time that pirates have attacked a cruise ship in ten years.
3 More than 200 ships have suffered from pirate attacks since the beginning of the year.
4 It has been suggested that all cargo and cruise ships should be accompanied by security boats.

12B Bounty hunter

Idioms (money)

1 Seven years ago Jayne Bingley didn't have a penny to her name. She was living from hand to mouth and struggling to pay the rent at the end of the month. Now she lives in the lap of luxury and has money to burn. It all began when a friend introduced her to eBay. She began with 20 dollars and some bits of old furniture. Now her antiques company is making millions and she's worth a fortune. 'It's a gold mine,' she said. 'I started out in the red and eBay was like a miracle cure. If you've got something to sell, there's always somebody out there who's ready to buy it.'

Passive reporting structures

2 1 are known to have been
2 it has been rumoured that
3 they were reported to have crossed
4 it is now believed that
5 it is thought that
6 who were said to have spoken
7 who were believed to be

3
1. *It has been reported that* the Sundance Kid never shot or killed anyone.
2. *It was rumoured that* they were often accompanied by a woman.
3. She went by the name of Etta Place, though *this is believed to have been* a false name.
4. *They were said to be* very polite and gentlemanly.
5. In Argentina, *they were rumoured to be* in trouble with the law.
6. *It has been suggested that* they returned to a life of crime because they were bored.

Translation
4 Translate the text into your language. Check with your teacher.

12C Scam

Phrasal verbs 2
1 5, 4, 2, 6, 8, 1, 3, 7

2 1 turned away   2 fell for   3 hand back
4 ripped / off   5 made up   6 give away

Causative
3 1 to do   2 cleaned   3 cooked   4 delivered
5 to come   6 massaged   7 to do   8 brought
9 to decide

💿 Dictation
4 💿 **35**
1. I'd love to have my whole life turned around.
2. I'd really like to get someone to show me how to manage my time.
3. I've always wanted to have my hair dyed blonde.
4. I wish I could get someone to help me with my accounts.

12D Dollar bill

Generalizing
1
1. People worry more about money than their health, general<u>ly</u> speaking
2. <u>On</u> the whole, pensioners are much better at keeping within their budgets than young people.
3. People carry less cash on them, <u>in</u> general, than they did ten years ago
4. As <u>a</u> rule, supermarket shoppers prefer to pay by credit card than in cash.
5. For <u>the</u> most part, shops and restaurants are happy to accept all major credit cards.
6. People only use cash for minor purchases by <u>and</u> large, such as a cup of coffee, a newspaper or a bus ticket.

US & UK English
2 ACROSS
2 garbage can 5 underground 6 sidewalk
11 aubergine 12 faucet
DOWN
1 petrol station 3 pants 4 vest 5 underpass
7 subway 8 waistcoat 9 check 10 soccer

3 1 garbage can   2 aubergine   3 soccer   4 faucet
5 check   6 pants

Translation
4 Translate the joke into your language. Check with your teacher.

12 Reading
1 *Students' own answers*

2 3

3 1 c   2 a   3 c   4 a   5 b

4 a 2   b 7   c 5   d 4   e 1   f 6   g 3

💿 Read & listen
5 💿 **36** Refer to Reading 12 *The Pharoah's Curse* on page 75.

Writing answer key

1A Applying for a job (1)

Language focus
1 1 I translated over 2,000 <u>R</u>ecipes from Spanish to English for a web-based recipe book, *La Cocina Española*. The <u>J</u>ob involved liaising with my co-writer, Jane Goode, and the <u>E</u>ditors responsible for the <u>P</u>roject.

2 I am a highly motivated and enthusiastic <u>G</u>raphic <u>D</u>esign <u>S</u>tudent. I am looking for an initial placement in a dynamic work environment.

3 rock-climbing: I was an active member of the outdoor pursuit club at <u>S</u>chool and have been interested in <u>R</u>ock <u>C</u>limbing ever since.

2 1 Work experience   2 Personal profile   3 Interests

3 1 b   2 a   3 c   4 a   5 c   6 b   7 c   8 a
9 c

4 1 successful   2 experience   3 professional
4 personal   5 voluntary   6 responsibilities
7 essential   8 knowledge   9 referees

5 1 c   2 d   3 b   4 f   5 a   6 e

6 1 chef   2 personal assistant   3 teacher
4 shop assistant   5 film critic   6 museum curator

7 1 was an active member of   2 duties included
3 am experienced in   4 helping other people with their work   5 at first   6 am looking for

1B Applying for a job (2)

Reading
1 1 voluntary work with an animal rescue shelter
2 no

2 1 F   2 T   3 T   4 F   5 T   6 F

Language focus
1 1 c   2 a   3 f   4 h   5 b   6 g   7 d   8 e

2 a 2   b 1   c 8   d 7   e 5   f 6

Writing

1 *Sample answer:*

Dear Sir or Madam,

I'm writing in response to your advertisement in *The Daily News* on January 23ʳᵈ for vacancies on your summer cruises. I am currently working as a part-time receptionist in a tourist complex in the North of Italy. I am interested in the positions you are offering as they would enable me to extend my experience in the holiday industry.

I have worked as a waitress, chef's assistant and receptionist in various hotels and restaurants in the Italian Dolomites and on the Adriatic coast over the last two and a half years, and have enjoyed the work atmosphere as well as the chance to meet new people. I would be very interested in working for your organization, as it would give me an opportunity to widen my horizons, both personally and professionally.

I have included a copy of my CV and the contact details for two referees. I will contact you early next week to discuss the next step in the selection process. Thank you for your time and consideration.

Yours faithfully,

Antonietta Rossi

2A A composition (1)

Language focus

1 3, 2, 1

2 1 c   2 a   3 b

3 1 synonymous with   2 favourite icons
3 the best known of   4 complete without
5 not the only   6 of which less than

4 a 1, 5, 4   b 6, 3, 2

5 1 argued   2 say   3 generally   4 reasonable
5 seems   6 feel   7 agree   8 doubt

6 *Students' own answers*

2B A composition (2)

Reading

1 3, 4, 1, 5, 2

2 4, 5, 2, 1, 3, 6

Language focus

1 1 from a young age   2 At the age of eleven
3 before long   4 From then on   5 Eleven years later
6 at 38 years of age

2 1 brief   2 why   3 famous   4 summary   5 early
6 how   7 grew

Writing

1 *Sample answer:*

Owain Glyndwr is unquestionably Wales's best loved hero. In the early 15th century he led a fifteen-year war against the English Crown and briefly established a Free Wales, for the first and only time in Welsh history.

Glyndwr was born to a noble Welsh family, and, as a young man he studied in London and fought for the English king. But when he married and returned to live in Wales, he found that the country was being tyrannized by English landowners. He led a revolt against a neighbour of his and was surprised by the depth and passion of the support he received from fellow Welshmen. This was the beginning of a rebellion which soon grew into a national guerrilla war.

By the end of 1403 Glyndwr controlled most of Wales. In 1404 he assembled a Parliament and drew up treaties with France and Spain. The war continued to rage until 1409 when the English armies regained control over the country and the rebellion was finally defeated. No one knows what happened to Owain Glyndwr. The new king twice offered Glyndwr a pardon, but apparently he was too proud to accept.

3A A review (1)

Language focus

1 a in   b of   c of   d by   e in   f in

2 1 adaptation   2 story   3 convincing   4 perfection
5 worthy   6 stars

3 1 It tells the story
2 The best moment in the whole movie
3 Most of the action
4 The cast has no stars
5 in the lead role
6 the part
7 which featured
8 Its plot is

4 *Students' own answers*

3B A review (2)

Reading

1 mainly positive

2 4, 1, 6, 2, 5, 3

Language focus

1 1 b   2 c   3 a   4 e   5 d   6 f

2 *Students' own answers*

Writing

1 *Sample answer:*

ER is arguably the most successful drama series on American TV. The series centres on the emergency room in a fictitious general hospital in Chicago and follows the day-to-day lives of the medical staff, both on and off the ward. It has been running since 1994 and has been the springboard for a host of stars, most notably George Clooney, who worked on the show for five consecutive years.
The series is written by award-winning novelist Michael Crichton, a trained medic, who first wrote the opening episode more than 20 years before it was finally broadcast. Although viewers dispute the accuracy of the medical treatments and procedures, the show is watched and loved by doctors and non-doctors alike, and the suspense and drama of the storylines keep it at the top of the TV ratings, year after year.

4A Writing to a friend

Language focus

1 4, 6, 10, 2, 3, 9, 7, 5, 8, 1

2 1 doing 2 nice 3 quick 4 too 5 again
6 call 7 last 8 now

3 1 Do you fancy going
2 I'm writing to invite you to
3 request the pleasure of your company
4 What about coming round to my place
5 We were wondering if you would like to
6 We would be very pleased if you could join us

4 a 1 b 4 c 6 d 2 e 3 f 5

5 *Sample answers:*

1

> Jo
>
> Are you doing anything this evening? We're going to that new Thai place. Do you fancy coming too?

2

> Hi everyone!
>
> Sorry for sending a circular email, but I'm incredibly busy at the moment. Brad and I are getting married! We're looking at dates and stuff at the moment and we'll let you know dates and venues and things once it's all decided.
>
> Love from both of us,
>
> Brad and Jo

3

> Dear Mr Jones,
>
> I am writing to you further to our discussion earlier this week. Would you be able to attend a meeting at 9am next Friday? If not, could you please suggest a time that would be convenient for you?
>
> Regards,
>
> Will Smith

4

> Dear Alex
>
> Many thanks for your email. We'd be delighted to come to the party. It'll be great to catch up with everybody. Do you know of any good B&Bs nearby? We fancy making a weekend of it.
>
> All the best,
>
> Sue.

4B Writing to a friend (2)

Reading

1 1 a 2 c 3 b 4 d

2 1 d 2 a 3 b 4 c

Language focus

1 I've gone to my appointment with the dentist. It won't take long. I'll see you when I get back. I should be back at about 6 at the latest. Love, Tracy.

2 1 Gone to meet Sam at the pub. Will be there until 9. Come and join us!
2 Thanks for the message. Really nice to be back at home. Huw is such a good baby, eating and sleeping really well and we can't take our eyes off him!
3 Thanks for your card. Doctors say things are going well. Should be home end of next week. Say hello to everyone at the office. Kay.
4 Thanks for the postcard. Glad your back's getting better. All looking forward to seeing you at work next week! Enjoy the rest of your holiday! Rod

3 A 4 B 1 C 2 D 3

Writing

1 *Sample answers:*
1 Can't sorry. Got to work late. C x
2 Bad luck! We'll miss you! Take care, Bob
3 Congratulations! Great news! Best of luck to the three of you!
4 Having a great time, loads to do and see, will tell you all about it when I get back. Jen x

5A A story (1)

Language focus

1 1 her 2 he 3 He 4 her 5 her 6 He
7 They 8 he 9 him 10 their 11 them
12 They

2 three students, the youngsters, the unlucky trio, the boys, the three friends

3 the rescue team, the helicopter crew, the emergency services

4 1 c the families of the three boys
2 e the emergency services
3 f local newspaper reporters
4 b the boys' friends
5 a the rescue team
6 d the helicopter crew

5 2 'You should always make sure you've got a full tank of fuel before you set out on a boat trip – no matter how short,' the emergency services warned/said.
3 'How did you feel when you realized you were drifting out to sea?' asked the local newspaper reporters.
4 'When they didn't turn up for the party, we phoned the coastguard,' said the boys' friends.
5 'When we found them, they were cold and frightened,' said the rescue team.
6 'It was hard work flying in those conditions – but it's all part of the job,' explained/said the helicopter crew.

5B A story (2)

Reading
1 1 C   2 A   3 B
2 1 B   2 A   3 C

Language focus
1 A conductor grabbed his jacket and pulled him back onto the train. The conductor said, 'You're lucky I saw you. Don't you know this train doesn't stop here?'

2 1 A man returned from shopping to find his car had been badly dented.
2 As he walked up to his car, he saw a note that had been left on his windscreen.
3 A man was waiting to pay at the supermarket when he noticed an elderly lady staring at him.
4 Because he felt sorry for her, he agreed to do it. / He agreed to do it because he felt sorry for her.
5 He didn't want to be late, so when the train arrived at his station, he jumped out.
6 The cashier, who had heard him say goodbye to the old woman, ignored his protests.

Writing
1 *Sample answers:*
2 The four men got out of the car and ran away.
3 Feeling shaken, she tried to start the car, but the key didn't fit.
4 She drove to the police station to report the story.
5 There were the four men who had just reported that their car had been stolen by a lady holding a handgun.

6A A report (1)

Language focus
1 1 purpose   2 provide   3 view   4 follows
5 suitability   6 requested   7 following
8 consideration   9 suitable   10 view   11 sum
12 suggest

2 1 A, F   2 B, D   3 C, E

3 4, 3, 7, 2, 9, 8, 6, 5, 1

4 neighbouring – nearby   located – situated
overlooking – looking out over   offer – provide
spectacular – breathtaking   drive – car journey

5 1 Although   2 However   3 Despite   4 However,
5 despite   6 Although

Sample answers:
6 1 It is situated about six miles outside the town in its own extensive gardens.
2 The hotel offers a restaurant, a grill and an extensive bar menu. There is a play area for younger children and bikes for hire to explore the surrounding countryside.
3 In conclusion, I recommend this hotel for short breaks with or without children and as a great base for exploring the surrounding area.

6A A report (2)

Reading
1 a to organize a diving trip to Cocos Island
b length of stay in San José, how many days to charter the boat for

2 1 find out about hotels and guesthouses in San José.
2 five days/four nights on the boat
3 Harriet
4 book flights
5 Ken
6 find out about cheap transfer options

Language focus
1 1 agree   2 decide   3 discuss   4 opt   5 suggest
6 volunteer

2 1 discussion   2 disagreement   3 decided
4 suggestion   5 agreed   6 volunteered

Writing
1 *Sample answer:*
Blackwater Dive Club
Meeting: Cocos Island trip
Wednesday 8th 8.30

Harriet opened the meeting by saying that she thought the trip had been a great success, despite the airport strike. Everyone agreed, but Dave suggested that the air controllers strike had put a bit of a dampener on the trip with the initial ten-hour delay. He continued by suggesting that we should write a letter of complaint to the local newspaper about the strike. There was some discussion and disagreement, with some members seeing the letter as being unnecessary and possibly even damaging to the club. In the end it was agreed that Dave would write the letter in his own name.

Jo and Ken suggested that we write a thank-you letter to the crew of the 'Caribbean Star' and volunteered to write it and bring it to the next meeting for approval. There was some discussion as to what present we could send them with the letter. There were no ideas put forward but everyone agreed to go away and think about it for the next meeting.

Harriet then projected her photos of the trip on the computer screen and presented a copy for the club records. Dave asked if we could possibly make copies for all the members who went on the trip. Harriet agreed and Dave volunteered to prepare the copies for next week.

The next meeting will be held on Monday next week at 8pm. Ken will be screening his DVD of the trip.